This book is dedicated to my family and friends.

It's also dedicated to my Grandparents, Father, and other loved ones who have passed away. They have always provided me with the ability to walk the path of righteousness and to proceed with duty, commitment, and dedication. Unless we have forgotten about them, our dead are never truly dead.

They are to be commended.

Contents

Contents

Contents

Acknowledgements

Prof. SC Srivastava, my guide, advisor, and mentor until his death, was instrumental in the accomplishment of my Ph.D thesis and this book in general. He is entirely deserving of praise. I'd like to thank him for his ongoing help in the writing of the thesis, as well as for checking over the manuscript and offering crucial revision suggestions at various points. It was his sincere goal to publish the thesis in book form, as recommended by the professors who examined it; however, due to a variety of factors beyond our control, this did not happen at the time. His wish has motivated me to publish it as a book, and I am confident that this will be a fitting tribute to him.

I'm also grateful to the three professors from different universities who took the time to read, evaluate, and remark on the thesis. I appreciate their recommendation.

Last but not least, I'd like to express my gratitude to my parents, relatives, and friends, without whom none of this would have been possible.

INTRODUCTION

CHAPTER I

ORIGIN OF EXISTENTIALISM AND ITS PROBLEMS

Existentialism is an issue that has arisen of contemporary philosophy. It originated in Denmark, developed in Germany and matured in France. This philosophy repudiates all those philosophical principals who have accepted as a main subject of philosophical thinking, the external world and not the man. Existentialists' center of thinking is man and they consider existent human being as their subject of thinking in this world. Though all existentialists' philosophers are not one on the subject but they agree to some extent while discussing human existence that (1) man is free (2) and that man is responsible for himself.

As a movement of thought, existentialism reaches back for its origin into the 19th century to the Danish Theologian Soren Aabye Kierkegaard, and to the strange German genius Friedrich Wilhelm Nietzsche but it crystallized out in the forties and fifties of this century in France. There are various reasons why existentialism coming from Germany where Karl Jaspers and Martin Heidegger developed it, as did JP Sartre and Gabriel Marcel in France appealed to such a wide stratum of intellectuals.

Existentialism emerged from the despair of a radical protestant thinker, Soren Aabye Kierkegaard, against "the shallow and barren Christianity of recent times. It came into being with emphasis on individual existence. It came with the gist of all existence, the self-based and harmoniously unfolding personality."[1]

Existentialism is generally opposed to the modern scientific rationalist and empiricist doctrine that assume that the universe is a determined, ordered system intelligible to the contemplative observer who can discover the natural laws that govern all beings and the role of reason as the power guiding human activity.

In the existentialist view, the problem of being must take precedence over that of knowledge, in philosophical investigations. Being can't be made a subject of objective enquiry; it is revealed to the individual by reflection on his own unique concrete existence in time and space. Existence is basic; it is the fact of the individual presence and participation in a changing and potentially dangerous world. Each individual understands his own existence in terms of his own experience of himself and of his situation. The self of which he is aware, is a thinking being who has beliefs, hopes, fears, desires, the need to find a purpose and a will. The problem of existence can have no significance if viewed in abstraction. It can be only seen in terms of the impact, the experiences made on a particular existent. No individual has a pre-determined place or function within a rational system and no one can deduce his supposed duty through reasoning. Everyone is compelled to assume the responsibility of making choices. Man is in a state of anxiety arising from the realization of his necessary freedom of choice, of his ignorance of the future, of his awareness of manifold possibilities and of the finiteness of an existence that was preceded by and must terminate in nothingness.

Existentialist thinkers distinguish between "authentic and inauthentic" form of existence. Some make the distinction on the basis of the individual's endeavour to transcend a particular situation, alternative being a denial of liberty and abandonment to a form of anonymity as a creature of circumstances. Others deny the possibility of transcending one's own point of view and claim that moral life is an illusion. Authenticity is the preservation of an individual's personal identity which is in danger of being eroded by deception under the influence and demands of society. Yet others regard the recognition of other free individuals and communication with them as a criterion of authentic existence.

Existentialists' thinkers share a common method, a common approach to problems. Thus, for all the existentialists, it is the individual human being who is of central importance and it is the "lived experience" of the individual that is the touchstone of all knowledge. This means the rejection of all "systematic" thought of the abstract and of the necessary and the universal for the sake of the particular and singular and unique experience of the individual.

Existentialists' have insisted upon the irreducible uniqueness of man. For them the world of human freedom stands over against the world of scientific determinism and can never be reduced to it. Existentialism has been an abnormally powerful fertilizing force in the intellectual culture of our times and that it cannot be dismissed as a passing vogue or fashion.2

Existentialism is forced to be centrally concerned with problems of human existence, Freedom and responsibility. It is not a movement or a set of ideas or an established list of authors. It is an "attitude which has found and is still finding philosophical expression in the most gifted writers of our time.”3

CHAPTER II

KINDS OF EXISTENTIALISM

Contemporary existentialist philosophy has developed in a great variety of ways. In France, Jean Paul Sartre and his followers are atheistic; Gabriel Marcel of France is a Roman Catholic. In Germany, Martin Heidegger is an atheist who has deeply influenced Christian thinkers. Karl Jaspers is a theist and in general way religious, though not a Christian. All those who are Christian or religious accept at least some of Kierkegaard's thought who is a theist. Friedrich Nietzsche is an atheist.

JP Sartre, in his book, Existentialism, writes, "There are two kinds of existentialists; first, those who are Christian; among whom, I would include Karl Jaspers and Gabriel Marcel, both catholic; and on the other hand, the atheistic existentialists, among whom I class Heidegger and then the French existentialist and myself.4

Thus, in a broad sense, Existentialism can be classified under two heads, first, the theistic or religious existentialism and, second, an atheistic existentialism.

Kierkegaard, Karl Jaspers and Gabriel Marcel, all religious thinkers, together, prepare the base for a theistic existentialism. And likewise, Martin Heidegger, Friedrich Nietzsche, and JP Sartre, together, build a strong foundation for atheistic existentialism.

Theistic existentialism is usually regarded as beginning with Soren Kierkegaard and atheistic existentialism with Friedrich Nietzsche as its pioneers.

Kierkegaard: - The theist sets many of the themes of existentialism. Specially, he puts an emphasis on the individual, the importance of subjectivity and anguish as the central emotion of human life, the need for a "leap of faith".

Gabriel Marcel: - A theistic existentialist, is a Roman Catholic. He denies having a philosophy that belongs exclusively to him, and which can be put into cut and dried form. His philosophy is a philosophy of second thoughts, a reflection upon reflection, not raising reflection to a higher degree of abstraction but using reflection to restore concreteness, the unity of living and thinking.

Karl Jaspers: - A theistic existentialist, denied being an existentialist or having any connection with Heidegger. Nonetheless he built his existential philosophy around the idea of authenticity, likewise stressing man's freedom and historicity.

Nietzsche: - The first atheistic existentialist, contributed to the movement the theme that "God is dead" and that each individual must seek his own values, providing a bridge to the future.

Heidegger: - An atheistic existentialist, is regarded as one of the most important of the existentialists. He stressed man's freedom authenticity, and nothingness.

JP Sartre: - Another atheistic existentialist, brings together all of the themes of authentic existentialism. Man's radical freedom and his responsibility, the death of God; the invention of values, authenticity, the presence of anguish and nothingness as a basic category.

In philosophical terms, every object has an essence, and an existence; an essence, that is to say, a certain effective presence in the world. Many people believe that essence comes first, and existence afterwards. This idea originates in religious thought (Theistic Existentialism). In fact, whoever wants to build house must know precisely what kind of object he is going to create. For all those who believe that God creates man; Essence precedes existence,[2] but even those who have no faith, have conserved the traditional opinion that the object never exists in conformity with its essence, and the whole 18th century believed that there was an essence common to all men, which they called human nature. Existentialism maintains, on the contrary, that with man alone- Existence precedes essence.[*]

In fact, what an individual will be is not rigidly predetermined in the embryo which contains its possibilities. Being free, man can choose among these possibilities not only by a first option, at his birth or at the awakening of his most powerful thought, but every day. The essence of the human being is in suspense in his liberty.[**]

Man chooses his essence; what essence? Not having distinguished between the universal essence, which makes us man, and the individual essence, that makes us this or that[***] particular man-timid or brave, honest or dishonest.

---

*Quoting JP Sartre, Paul Foulqui in his book, existentialism, writes-In man, Existence precedes essence.

The very word existentialism indicates recognition of a certain priority or primary of existence in relation to essence, not in things in general, but only in man.

(Existentialism, Paul Foulqui, P. 47....)

** Being and nothingness, JP Sartre, P.61

*** JP Sartre in 'Action' said that this means more simply, that man first is, and that afterwards he is this or that (JP Sartre in Action, Dec 12th 44).

Obviously, we do not create the universal or specific essence in virtue of which we belong to the human species, but the individual essence which is peculiar to each of us, is not be found in any other human being. Our generic and specific essence- "animal" and" man"- is not determined by us; we are man only; our individual or specific essence presents a certain indetermination. Never the less, there remains a considerable scope for choice.

Besides, if I cannot choose the social class into which I am born, my height, or my intelligence, or my attitude that I adopt toward this crude fact depends upon myself. The proletarian is " totally conditioned by his class", but it is he who decides upon the meaning of his condition, and that of his comrades; is he who freely decided; for the proletariat, upon a future of unrelieved humiliation, or on conquest and victory, according as he chooses to be resigned, or to be a revolutionary.* I am an invalid without having chosen to be so ; but' I cannot be an invalid...... without choosing the way in which I regard my infirmity (as 'intolerable', 'humiliating', 'to be concealed', 'to be exhibited to all', as ' a source of pride' as ' a justification for my failures, etc.). 'I chose to be myself, not in my being, but in my manner of being'.** Now the attitude that I adopt towards what I am, contributes towards transforming me. This attitude constitutes in a region that seemed to the independent of me, a door opens upon liberty.[5]

---

*Ibid

**Being and nothingness, JP Sartre, P.393, 633

CHAPTER III

DETERMINISM AND LIBERTY

Determinism is the doctrine that all events are the inevitable result of antecedent conditions and that the human beings, in acts of apparent choice show the mechanical expression of their heredity and the past environment.

Determinism argues that a given future event must either occur or not occur. Whichever happens will turn out to be correct, and therefore was correct all along, whether or not we know it.

KINDS OF DETERMINISM: -

Determinism is sometimes divided into hard and soft. Hard determinist says that our actions are caused in a way that makes us not as free as we might have thought, so that responsibility if it implies free will, is an illusion. The causes may be physical and psychological (events in the brain) or else mental (e.g., conscious or unconscious desires, and childhood experiences which cause such desires). Hard determinists are incompatibilities i.e., think freewill and universal causation are incompatible.

Soft determinists, by far the largest class in recent times, say that our actions are indeed caused but we are not therefore any less than we might be, because the causation is not a constraint or collusion on us. So long as our natures and choices are affecting as items in the causal chain, the fact that they are themselves caused is irrelevant and does not stop them being what they are.

Soft determinists often hold that what justifies praise and blame is solely that they can influence action. Soft determinists are compatibilists i.e., think freewill and universal causation are compatible.[6]

Liberty or freewill is the partial freedom of the agent in acts of conscious choice from the determining compulsion of heredity environment, and circumstances.

Liberty and determinism are two apparently opposed philosophical concepts, "the former postulating that man is able to choose and act according to the dictates of his own will, the latter that all events including human actions are predetermined. We cannot but assume in most everyday life on many occasions we are free agents, able to do or to abstain from doing this or that at will". *

Everything, including human conduct really happens with the absolute inevitability. The philosophical problem is to discover what the presuppositions and implications of the two areas actually are and whether they can or cannot be reconciled. Adherents of the one view, as mentioned, are compatibilists, and of the other incompatibilists.

If the doctrine of theistic creation is true, then can this leave any room for human responsibility and choice? In the theistic context, it is usual to speak of predestination, implying that everything including particularly every choice has been fixed in advance by divine decree.[7]

- A dictionary of Philosophy, Antony Flew, P.125

CHAPTER IV

MEANING OF HUMAN LIBERTY

Certainly, one of the most basic meaning of freedom centers on the idea of significant choice. In this sense freedom means the power of selecting any of the two or more alternatives. If we have the power to do other than we have done in most of the situations which confront us in life then we are free in this sense. If one holds this view of freedom, it is natural to think of the future as open or indeterminate. Hence, indeterminism is a natural corollary of this view of freedom.

The existentialists generally hold to a most extensive freedom of choice. JP Sartre stresses the human ambivalent attitude towards freedom, its vast extent in human life and the escapist character of doctrine of determinism.

CHAPTER V

KINDS OF LIBERTY

In this regard we can have two stands

1. Whether human being is free in his choice of action or
2. Are his actions preordained by forces beyond his control and opposed to his will?

If we say that man is free, how can we reconcile our answer with our acknowledgement of objective necessity?

If we say he is not free, does this mean that people are only a means of realizing the laws of social development? According to Kant, if human acts of will are empirically conditioned and necessary, no human being can be held responsible for them. That is why Kant maintains that there may be contradiction between freedom and necessity in one and the same human actions. In pronouncing his final verdict on the human beings, Kant states that although you as a human being acted thus because you could not act otherwise, your actions being conditioned by circumstances and consequently you are not to be blamed. It does not matter whether, after all, you could or could not have acted, and otherwise you are still guilty, since you should not have acted as you did.

According to Kant, the ability to initiate events independently (i.e., without compulsion) is freedom, man has many roads before him and he can choose any one of them.

Freedom is sometimes defined only in a negative sense, as personal independence, as the ability to say "no". However, every denial has to be made from certain, perhaps not fully conscious position, implying a positive principle, which justifies a person's rejection of something and expresses the meaning and value of his rejection. Any rejection of one thing must imply an assertion of something else.

Freedom is a specifically human mode of existence and only the realization of freedom can be good in the human sense. One cannot live in society and be free of society.

The individual is not free always to act as he sees fit. He must co-ordinate his actions with those of the people around him. It is his responsibility to correlate his behavior with their interests and activities. He is compelled to suppress some of his feelings and impulses and channelize them in different directions from what he may have wished.

When speaking of freedom, one should not think of it as doing anything one like's i.e., whimsical arbitrariness such freedom simply does not exist. Human actions are restricted by various factors, legal, moral, aesthetics and by various traits of character, natural abilities and so on. According to Sartre, 'Freedom is autonomy of choice'. It is realized where a person initiates his own desires, chooses on his own behalf, and on behalf of the self.

Man's free fulfillment of goals which he, as a rational being, sets himself, can be based only on utilization of the laws of nature and social reality, not on contempt for them. Consequently, freedom presupposes, above all, knowledge of laws that are not dependent on human beings, and it is this knowledge that makes people intrinsically free. Thus, freewill emerges as a concept closely related to the concepts of consciousness and knowledge. Knowledge is not only power; it is also freedom. The only path to freedom is the path to knowledge. Ignorance is shared for bondage. The degree of knowledge determines the degree of freedom. One cannot desire what one does not know. Knowledge in itself is not yet freedom, but there can be no freedom without it. Freedom implies not only knowledge of the condition and laws of development in the present but also preparation of the future result of conscious activity, their prevision. Both personal and social freedom consists not in some imagined independence of objective laws, but in the ability to actively chose and take decision with knowledge of the case and, above all, to think and act in conditions that make it possible to realize one's intentions.

The concept of freedom as conscious necessity is essential but is only the first step on the road to an understanding of the nature of freedom. It allows us to distinguish freedom from arbitrariness and stresses the priority of objective conditions.

According to Jaspers, the freest people of all are insane, because they have no logic, Existentialism interprets the human being as a force standing in opposition to the world and hostile to it.

Man is free not from nature, not from society and their laws but within the framework provided by the operation of both the laws of nature and society. When they are known, they make a person's will relatively free. But they also determine its limits. The limits to the realization of goals that man set himself; free will is not, arbitrariness.

Freedom is the ability, based on knowledge of necessity, to choose and to act in accordance with this necessity. It consists not only in knowledge of natural and social laws but also in the practical realization of this knowledge. Realization of freedom presupposes the overcoming of certain obstacles and the more difficult the obstacle the stronger and more freedom loving the will must be.

Freedom lies not only in the choice of a certain aim from a number of possibilities, but also in creativity in the settings of new goals. Freedom is not only conscious necessity, but also the existence created by the human beings themselves, his social relations, the world of material and intellectual culture.

The idea freedom is wholly human and social, it differs in every concrete historical set of circumstances. In itself freedom is an abstraction. As a reality it is always full of concrete historical meaning. Freedom is a historically developing thing, a process of development that is never fully realized. Nature knows no freedom.[8]

CHAPTER VI

HUMAN RESPONSIBILITY

The existentialists absolutise the individual's responsibility to society believing that every person is responsible for everything that happens in the world. This thesis is based on the premise that the individual will is independent of the flow of historical events and that these events are the product of individual will. Every separate person is responsible for everything because this "everything" is consciously created by him, but this is subjective idealism. It is vividly expressed, for example, in Sartre, who maintains that man, being condemned to freedom, assume the weight of the whole world on his shoulders; he is responsible for the world and for himself.

Responsibility expresses society's specific demand on the individual in the form of duty. There are certain social standards but there is also freedom of choice, including the possibility of violating those standards. Where there is no choice, there is no responsibility. The individual becomes aware of his personal responsibility when he knows what other people expect of him. Responsibility may appear in two forms, retrospective and actual, i.e., responsibility for previously performed actions and for actions that are being performed at the given moment.

Responsibility is a state of consciousness, a feeling of duty towards society and oneself, an awareness of the purpose of the actions performed and their consequences for a certain social group or class and oneself. Responsibility is society's necessary means of controlling the behavior of the individual through his consciousness. As an integral attribute of the socially developed personality; Responsibility embodies all forms of the individual's activity in the moral, political, civic, legal and other spheres. There are no forms of non-responsible activity, in as much as there is no activity whose consequences do not affect the interests of the individual himself, the social group or society as a whole.

Historically, individual responsibility to society shows a tendency to increase in the wake of social progress. In contemporary society the importance of every individual's civil, political and moral responsibility to society, his responsibility for the fate of nations and of all humanity has sharply increased. The individual is responsible to the extent that he is free in his actions. The individual is generally free only in doing or achieving something that is the realization of his own intention. It is for this kind of action and achievement that the individual is responsible. He is not responsible and cannot be held responsible for what is done by others against his will. The blame for such actions cannot be laid at his door.

Responsibility and liability have meaning only in so far as they induce positive changes in the individual in relation to his future behaviour. Responsibility means much more than accountability. Inward responsibility for one's behavior and intentions, that is to say, self-control, self-appraisal, and the general regulation of one's life, is also of great importance.

An important form of responsibility is responsibility for the future, both near and distant, which is built on the sense of responsibility for the present and the past.

The character of responsibility and its forms have changed in the course of history. The tribal system knew no personal responsibility. There was responsibility only to the community, which imposed a certain course of action on its members and controlled these actions. The slave society revealed the beginning of a tendency towards individuality, while the commune fettered the action of the individual. The slave society allowed him to act at his own risk, with a certain degree of independence. During the slave-owning period the individual was responsible not to the community, nor yet to himself, but to the polity and to the gods. With the risk of the state the concept of individual responsibility to the state, the monarch and to God began to take shape.[9]

The real measure of responsibility that a person bears for his actions depends on the real conditions that life has granted him for consciously evaluating the consequences of his actions and taking a corresponding personal stand.

PART-I

HUMAN LIBERTY AND RESPONSIBILITY IN THEISTIC EXISTENTIALISM

HUMAN LIBERTY AND RESPONSIBILITY IN SOREN AABYE KIERKEGAARD'S PHILOSOPHY

CHAPTER VII

SOREN AABYE KIERKEGAARD(1813-1855): Brief Sketch and Introduction

Søren Aabye Kierkegaard (1813-1855)

Søren Aabye Kierkegaard

Born

Søren Aabye Kierkegaard, 5 May 1813, Copenhagen, Denmark–Norway

Died

11 November 1855 (aged 42),Copenhagen, Denmark

Education

University of Copenhagen,(M.A., 1841)

Region

Western philosophy

School

Existentialism, Continental philosophy, Christian existentialism, Existential psychology[1][2]

Thesis

Om Begrebet Ironi med stadigt Hensyn til Socrates (On the Concept of Irony with Continual Reference to Socrates) (1841)

Main interests

Aesthetics,Christianity,Epistemology,Ethics,Metaphysics,Philosophy of Christianity

Poetry, Psychology

Notable ideas

The Absurd, Angst, Authenticity, Existential despair, Existential philosophy,

Infinite qualitative

distinction, Knight of faith, Leap of faith, Present age

Influences

Abraham,Descartes,Diogenes,Hamann,Goethe,Hegel,Heiberg,
Kant,Lessing,Luther,
Mozart,Møller,Olsen, Plato,Schelling,Shakespeare[4],Socrates,Wolff[5].

Influenced

Adorno,Barth,Bergman,Buber,Camus,Caputo,Ellul,Freud,
Heidegger,Ibsen,Jaspers,
Kaufmann,Levinas,H. R. Niebuhr,Marcel[6],May,Merton,Percy,
Sartre,Schmitt,
Shestov,Tillich
Unamuno,Wahl,West,Wittgenstein

Courtesy -Wikipedia

SOREN AABYE KIERKEGAARD

Kierkegaard was born in 1813 in Copenhagen. His father was occupied after his retirement with theological and philosophical study and discussion. He was profoundly melancholy and exerted a powerful and somber influence upon Kierkegaard, communicating to the child his preoccupation with his own guilt and the most violent concept of the Christian faith. Kierkegaard later described this treatment as 'spiritual rape'.

Kierkegaard freed himself from the direct domination of his father and gave himself up to the intellectual and social influence of student life. He spent two years completing the theological studies which had become distasteful to him. Thereafter he went to Berlin in Germany, eager to hear Schelling lecture on the Hegelian system but was disappointed. He soon returned to Copenhagen. He wrote more than 20 publications. He died in Copenhagen in 1855 at the age of forty-two only.

INTRODUCTION

Soren Kierkegaard was the father of contemporary Existentialism. He was born in Copenhagen in 1813, and died in Copenhagen in 1855. It is impossible to understand his work without understanding a little of his life. As a young child, he was deeply influenced by the religion of his father. Later, as a young man, he threw off that influence as far as he could, and for a time, believed himself to have escaped entirely from it. He gave up his time to learning as much as he could of the world and to enjoying himself.

In 1836, he underwent a kind of moral conversion, and for a time lived his life in accordance with strict and universal moral principles. Then in 1838, he was converted to Christianity. Kierkegaard sharply distinguished the state through which he passed. His first emancipated years were called by him the authentic stage. At this time, he had seemed to himself to enjoy freedom, but this freedom turned out to be illusory. The higher stage to which he next passed on was also ultimately based upon on illusion, not, this time, the illusion of freedom, for in the ethical stage of life he felt himself bound by the laws of universal and absolute validity. The illusion was of 'humanism'; for the ethical laws which were the framework of his life had no transcendental backing, but were derived from human requirements, and fixed, social standards. Being converted from this stage to Christianity, he threw off the humanistic illusion, and finally adopted the standpoint of faith.

The illusion from which Kierkegaard himself, above all, wanted to free people was the illusion of objectivity. This was the illusion most likely not only in fact to dominate people's thought, but actually to be welcomed by them as enlightenment and progress. He says that "we have lost the capacity for subjectivity, and it is the task of philosophy to rediscover it for us."[1]

CHAPTER VIII

METHOD OF STUDY

Kierkegaard, exclusively, uses the subjective method of study. Here, I must consider what Kierkegaard means by 'objectivity' and 'subjectivity'. Objectivity shows itself in the tendency to accept rules governing both behavior and thought. Any subject matter which is bound by rules of evidence, or which can be taught in the class room, falls in the domain of objectivity.

Objectivity is the acceptance of the role of the observer who adopts or discovers general laws, but is not easy to discard objectivity. Subjectivity, paradoxical as it may seem, is hard to achieve.

The 'subjective method', ought to mean nothing more or less than a particular approach, of equal validity to the objective method to be used where objectivity is insufficient that is where personal participation is required for the gaining of any knowledge at all and in such cases, usually, we try to deal with personal experiences, morality, values, and faith. This implies, therefore, that the subjective method should be, in its own way, just as reliable as the objective.

Kierkegaard thus not only shows how fruitfully the method can be used, but reveals some of its main characteristics and thus helps us to apply it correctly.[2]

There are three essential characteristics of subjective knowledge. First, it cannot be passed on from one person to other, nor added to by different researchers. It cannot be taught in the class room. Second, what is known as subjectivity always has the nature of a paradox. For faith alone, and not reason, can induce us to accept paradox. Faith is not an intellectual, but an emotional attribute. Kierkegaard says, 'Christianity wishes to intensify passion (Deep feeling) to the highest pitch; but passion is subjectivity, and does not exist objectively. Third, subjective knowledge is concrete, not abstract. This is because it must necessarily be related to the actual concrete existence of a living individual.[3]

His starting point is the distinction between knowledge and faith. Knowledge, in this context means knowledge achieved by a conscious effort of thinking. His position is that everything which we can know is impossible to believe. This may sound like an exaggeration, but we can see what he means. Because we cannot acquire all the knowledge we need by our own efforts, we must, in practice, often believe others; yet in principle we could ourselves test all knowledge based on the objective method, we could, for instance, learn to make scientific experiments ourselves, so as to decide whether the conclusion based on them are acceptable, or we could look up the documents so as to see whether such statements as "Kierkegaard was born in Copenhagen in 1813 corresponds to the facts. Belief is only of secondary, practical importance. Yet with faith, belief is of the essence, because it refers to the divine sphere which transcends man and therefore cannot be fully known. Here we have to perform the act of faith; we need a constantly renewed willingness to accept what is beyond proof, we must risk the jump into the abyss' which can be justified not by a preceding knowledge of its results, but only by the ensuring experiences. Thus, faith is not, as is often assumed a week substitute for knowledge, to be replaced by it as soon as possible. The two are fundamentally different.

The subjective method should reveal a truth which, in contrast to factual information can become a personal experience and thereby have a deep influence upon what we believe and do-an influence such as is exercised by any kind of faith.

To discover the truth by which we live, we must start from personal experience and base our ideas on it not vice-versa. Kierkegaard's attempt to infer existence from thought is a contradiction. For thought takes existence away from the real and thinks it, by translating it into the sphere of the impossible. He illustrates this statement by discussing the equilateral triangle which never occurs in perfect geometrical regularity in nature; such regularity is achieved only when all actual natural conditions are disregarded.

We must start from our personal experience of existence. Such a start requires us to apply, constantly and correctly, the subjective method. Kierkegaard is aware of its difficulties; it is commonly assumed that no art or skill is required in order to be subjective. To be sure, every human being is a bit of a subject, in a sense. But now to strive to become what one already is; who would take the pains to waste his time on such a task, involving the greatest imaginable degree of resignation?...... But for this very reason alone it is very difficult task, the most difficult of all tasks in fact.

What the method itself means is perhaps best illuminated when Kierkegaard says "An objective acceptance of Christianity is the way of life; to accept it as an interesting line of thought, as an abstract explanation of the universe, or as ritual, but without acting upon it makes it well-nigh meaningless. The subjective method always establishes first the relationship between, life and action. To give reality to the creed, the method involves us in its consequences. We must be willing to commit ourselves to what we believe so as to understand its meaning through the actual experience. Actions will only produce the right kind of subjective insight, however, if they are based on the right attitude. Kierkegaard demands this attitude when he observes. 'The majority of men are subjective towards themselves, while being objective towards all others, terribly objective sometimes- But the real task is exactly the opposite; to be objective towards one self and subjective towards all others. We should not give in to our natural tendency to be severe towards others and lenient to ourselves, for we shall understand others only if we try to understand them from within, by attempting to make their experiences our own. When confronting ourselves, however, we need a certain detachment to enable us to distinguish bias and prejudice from that self which is common to all men, but becomes accessible through personal experience alone. In other words, we always need the contrast between objectivity and subjectivity; therefore, we have to believe to it both outside us, where objectivity seems more natural, and also inside us, where biased subjectivity tends to blind us. We need action because they create the relationship between outside and inside, and they will increase our understanding if both our objective and subjective attitude are right, God alone, according to Kierkegaard, is the absolute subjectivity'. For Him, outside and inside are one, and what appears objective and thus foreign to us, is known to him fully from within. We have to make objectivity serve the subjective method.

Most of the non-existentialist philosophers start from things then includes the person, but only as an abstract entity, as an abstract thinker, and return to things again, so as to gain objective knowledge. Kierkegaard starts from the person, and then includes the things, in order to gain and clarify personal experiences, and return to the person again, so as to achieve the right kind of subjectivity. He wants to turn our attention to inner experiences; his aim is inwardness.

There is, however, another contrast between the two methods; the reliability which each can achieve is different, because it is based on two different kinds of certainty.

The results of the objective method can be tested, proved, and once they are proven, satisfactorily communicated to others, because they can be accepted without further enquiry. Yet they are never final, although, the facts do not change their interpretation changes.

The subjective method remains dependent on constantly renewed experiences; its results cannot be accepted once and for all, because they always have to be translated into our own experiences. As personal participation is required an area of uncertainty must be left open, so as to allow for personal decisions. Thus, the application of this method is constantly beset by difficulties and danger; none of its results can be taken for granted. Yet once, certainty is achieved. It is absolute. When we fully experience goodness, for instance, we can no longer doubt that we have touched upon a reality which we must accept unconditionally, if we are to do justice to our experience; therefore, the results of the subjective method have the stability of the ten commandments or the sermon on the mount a stability unequalled in the sphere of the objective method. These results are final, yet they cannot be fully communicated; they must again and again be made our own experiences if they are to become our own conviction and part of our lives. Thus, there is always a risk, nothing prevents us from making the wrong decisions. But the risk is worth taking, for, while science can completely reshape the external form of our life, the possible positive results of the subjective method alone have a profound significance for our inner, personal development.[4]

CHAPTER IX

DENIAL OF BELIEF

Soren Kierkegaard, in his middle age underwent a moral conversion and lived his life in accordance with moral principles. Finally, he was converted to Christianity and adopted the stand point of faith. He made it the effort of his life to renew the meaning of Christianity by compelling recognition of the permanent cleavage between faith and reason.

Faith is usually defined as acceptance of truth on some other basis than reason. The belief is justified by events where faith is associated with religious belief, an alternative basis does intrude. Religious belief is not only faith as acceptance of what one has insufficient reason to believe, it can be faith as acceptance of what one has no reason to believe, and even of what one has sufficient reason not to believe.

Religious belief is often said to be supported by revelation, * whether the believer's own or that of some acknowledged authority, sometimes one on whose alleged testimony a whole institution has been erected. The presence of such institution can confuse the issue of the basis of religious belief. Given their influence a person might 'believe' simply through fear of consequences of not doing so, where the fear would be the same whatever the contest of the doctrine subscribed to, or through mistakenly taking the assistance of the institution as itself a good reason, in which case the doctrine has not been identified as especially religious. It seems essential when looking for the motivation and support for religious belief, that these be seen to attach to the content of the belief itself, that is, the belief represent some state of affairs which the believer would like to obtain, or to be presently obtaining, and that the support be understood as working independently of whatever evidential basis there is for believing that it does or that it does not obtain. Religious belief, then might be said to be acceptance of a preferred conclusion on some basis other that whatever is rational including observational.[5]

The decision of faith entails an ethical decision to renounce the world, to break off all attachments specially the most cherished ones. No more decision of faith can thus be externalized and made once for all (e.g., by retirement to a monastery). The believer goes on as before with no perceptible external difference, but the internal difference is total.

Everything is resigned, at the same time all that was formally enjoyed is still actually possessed and the desire for it is therefore accentuated. Resignation, possession, desires are equally read and daily renewed. This maintains an inner tension of suffering and passion which increases the tension of faith and reason.[6]

Kierkegaard's arguments deal with the object of Christian faith. He argues that a man born and living in history says that he is a God and dies in humiliation plunges into a dilemma those who would build their lives on him and his preaching's. Nothing has happened since to lighten by one scruple, the strain on belief.

The present generation is exactly in the position of the contemporaries of Christ who witnessed his humiliation on the cross. Faith, today, unless it is faith in the faith of the apostles, is not other than their faith in the man who makes the most absurd of claims. The truth of this claim cannot in the nature of the case be made objectively certain, or even investigated, on the contrary, the absolute discontinuity between the human and the divine which inheres in the concept of God makes it unthinkable, so that it cannot by any human mind be recognized as true, cannot be entertained as a possibility.

In Kierkegaard's view, "Christianity is most absurd. It is hard to believe that God becomes the lowliest of men and was executed. Still Jesus reflected the strongest possible act of faith".[7]

However, "Christianity is not a doctrine. It can be considered as an existence; Christianity is not the doctrine about denying oneself about this being but Christianity is to deny oneself. And if Christ, this moment was to express absolute self-denial, death would be certain".[8]

---

*Christian revelation had been naturalized, assimilated made probable and acceptable an inheritance reconciled with rest of history in a total world view. There is always an attempt to reconcile faith and reason, to philosophize Christian beliefs to graft revelation into the tree of natural theology. Sooner or later comes the extrusion of Christian belief as wholly alien to reason and experiences, incapable of assimilation a limit and a challenge to thought. Such a movement of thought may spring from the tension between a skeptical mind and a religious heart, but it represents also the persistent tension between Christian dogma and secular creatures. (Six cxistentialist thinkers, H.J. Black ham P.3)

CHAPTER X

HUMAN NATURE

Kierkegaard's thought on human nature can be stated briefly, taking into account the finite and infinite characteristics of man. Man as a human being always shares his humanity with others. He forms certain ideals and standards of human nature. The ideals and standards can be attained through his attention toward his duty and righteousness. Man, who has been distinguished as "good man" will always try consistently to choose the right kind of ideals and standards, which would finally benefit his oneself and other selves. All these forms the finite characters of a man. Apart from this he also strives to cultivate his infinite characters needed to exalt his personality.

Man in itself is divided into the self and the soul. The self is a synthesis in which the finite is limiting factor and the infinite, the expanding factor. The soul is expressing the expanding side when it realizes that it exists and that its existence is its infinite concern. But this concern is not one. It can cope with by itself; it can be performed only by means of a relationship to God.

Man is synthesis of the infinite and the finite, of the temporal and the eternal, of freedom and necessity, in short, he is a synthesis.

A person can remain in his freedom only by constantly realizing it. He realizes it by choosing to choose. This choice is transcendent and refers not to the reality of things chosen, but to the reality of the act of choice. I do not choose this or that thing primarily; I chose myself, to see and be myself.

For the choice being made with the whole inwardness of his personality, his nature is purified and he himself brought into immediate relation to the external power whose omnipresence interpenetrates the whole of existence.

The aesthetical in a man is that by which he is immediately what he is, the ethical that whereby he becomes what he becomes. The great thing is not this or that but to be oneself and this everyone can do if he wills it. The choice itself is decisive factor for the content of the personality. The instant of choice is very serious. 'Only a serious personality is a real personality'.

Summarizing, I can firmly say that man, who is a synthesis of finite and the infinite, * as mentioned above, is never complete without the synthesis.

He has to live but a half-life rather an incomplete living. In absence of this synthesis, he will be deprived of expressing his full personality. He will cease to be a man. He will become inactive. He will lose the power of making choices; and possibly he will disintegrate. Since he loses to be a man; he also, for the want of synthesis, exhibits his incomplete human nature. Consequently, his cultivation of infinite characteristics comes to a grinding halt; and his complete progress is checked, and he stops to grow as a full human being.

---

*Man is a synthesis of the finite and the infinite......in short, he is a synthesis. (Sickness unto death- Soren Kierkegaard Tr. By Walter Lowrie, Princeton University Press, 1941, P.17)

CHAPTER XI

HUMAN LIBERTY

The existent individual, as Kierkegaard defines him, is first of all he who is in an infinite relationship with himself and has an infinite interest in himself and his destiny. Secondly, the existent individual always feels himself to be in becoming with a task before him; and applying this idea to Christianity, Kierkegaard says, one is not Christian one becomes Christian. It is a matter of sustained effort. Thirdly, the existent individual is excited with a passionate thought; he is inspired; he is a kind of incarnation of the infinite in the finite. This passion which animates the existent (and this brings us to the fourth characteristics) is what Kierkegaard calls "the passion of freedom".

According to Kierkegaard, A man who is converted is shown that he is free. In the first place he is free to choose whether to move from one stage of enlightenment to another. This is the primary exercise of freedom, and if men were not free, they could not be enlightened, since accepting the true state of affairs is an act of a concrete individual which cannot be done on his behalf by anyone but himself. If I try to accept the truth on your behalf, then I have misunderstood the nature of truth. The truth exists for you and it exists for me, but each of us must grasp it for himself. This is what 'inwardness' amounts to.

Secondly, men are free because they are able to think for themselves, and need not have recourse to laws, to rules, nor to the standards of History and Science. This freedom is identical with isolation. If one is entirely alone on a desert island then, though one may not be free in all senses of the word, there is an important sense in which one is free. It is not enough to live long; we must know how to live well. For this, man has to decide his way of living. All the props of civilization, the supports of morality, the law the institutionalized religion and learning have been removed. It is in this desert island sense that Kierkegaard's man of faith is free. He is self-governing and more than that, he is creative. Nothing on his island is valuable unless he makes it so. If he comes trailing relics of accepted values, codes, or rules behind him, then he is not a moral man. His morality lies precisely in the fact that he is discovering the truth for himself, is inwardness.

It is the 'existential value' of freedom which determines the worth of one's action, that is, an action is of 'Existential value', if it is the result of a freely chosen commitment. Free choice is the mark of the "truly existent individual", setting him off from the "crowd", a clearly derogatory term in Kierkegaard's writings, why is it valuable to be a truly existent individual as opposed to a member of the crowd? Why should it be better to suffer the despair and anxiety which accompanies one's recognition of freedom? Freedom is not a measure of the value of one course of action as opposed to another, but a measure of the value of a person in choosing some course of action.

This question of the value of freedom is to become, in later existentialist thinkers like Sartre, the Central problem of their philosophical thinking, JP Sartre, for example, sees as Kierkegaard does not, that there is at least an apparent inconsistency in denying the existence of absolute values and maintaining that the only value is freedom. Where Sartre attempts to dispel the problem, Kierkegaard does not even recognize that there is problem. Similarly, there is a multitude of well-established doctrines in philosophy which would deny that there is even a single case of freedom of choice. Kierkegaard makes virtually no mention of the 'free will problem', but simply assumes the reality of the individual freedom he values. Kierkegaard's most sympathetic interpreters have suggested that his concept of freedom does have a basis in his phenomenological description of our experience of freedom, and that this description establishes both the actuality of this freedom and the value of it. The problem of whether one actually has free choice is fully distinct from the question of how we feel when we believe that we have free choice. And Kierkegaard has virtually nothing to say about this problem, nor does he seem to be the least bit interested in it. Freedom, for Kierkegaard, is simply 'suggested' as value in "persuasive-definition" of the "truly existing individual" or the "authentic human being" as one who recognizes the ultimate value of freedom, choice, and passion.[11]

CHAPTER XII

HUMAN RESPONSIBILITY

Kierkegaard lays great emphasis on freedom and responsibility. According to him these are the true essences of subjectivity which in turn is the essence of man. He writes, "The truth of a situation is only grasped when it is seen from within, by those who are living through it". It follows from this that truth is subjective and brings responsibility with it. He holds himself responsible for his acts, he says "for as soon as I have to act, interest or concern is laid upon me because I take responsibility on myself, and thereby acquire importance".

Kierkegaard, being the first theistic existentialist opines that "the authentic individual is not only responsible to himself and his fellowmen; he is above all responsible to God". The ethical mode of life is transformed into the religious mode of life when with a contrite heart, man chooses himself as guilty and hopes for divine forgiveness, "there is an "either/or" which makes a man greater than angles". *

The ethical and the religious aspects of existence are usually combined in the philosophy of Kierkegaard so as together to constitute the level of human existence. This combination is based upon his conception of the self with a polar nature. The self is a synthesis of the finite and the infinite, the temporal and eternal. The self knows itself to be such a synthesis when it chooses itself in its authentic existence. ** As finite and temporal, it relates itself to its fellow beings in the world through the performance of moral actions with sincerity and consistency, but as striving towards eternal happiness, it relates itself to God through bonds of commitment. In fact, man copes with his ethical responsibility mainly because of his relationship with God acquired through faith. His religious consciousness of inward relationship with God penetrates his concrete living in the world and sustains his actions at the ethical level so that they will be universally acceptable and applicable.

But an important line of distinction is sometimes drawn by Kierkegaard within the ethico-religious stage between the ethical and the religious. The ethical rule, according to him is always universal, something which all must follow; but the religious man may have to break it sometimes, make an exception of himself, if he is called upon to do so by God.

The exceptional individual who is called upon to dedicate his entire life to the cause of religion or God must give it preference over the performance of ethical acts. Kierkegaard thus affirms the superiority of the religious and the 'individual' over the ethical and the universal and this is the distinguishing features of Kierkegaard's philosophy. The ethical life is to be perused on the basis one's religious commitment to God but on no account, should be regarded as a 'Substitute' for it. The individual must invariable choose the religious in preference to the 'ethical' if he is called upon to do so.

Thus, we see that Kierkegaard's concept of authentic existence is fundamentally religious and that is why he holds man responsible to God.

---

*Refers-The Existentialist Revolt, Kurt F. Reinhardt, New York 1912, P.56

** Kierkegaard has described the authentic existence in his doctrine of the stage and works of love, "the self exists authentically when it becomes free to shoulder its responsibility and open itself for a commitment, religiously defined as a commitment to god who commands a resolute love of one's neighbor. (Existence and freedom towards an Ontology of human finitude, Calvin O. Schrage, P. 49)

CHAPTER XIII

CONSEQUENCES OF HUMAN LIBERTY AND RESPONSIBILITY

Kierkegaard is concerned only with a particular kind of existence, namely, individual human existence. Kierkegaard speaks of individual existence in a very special sense, a sense in which a man is not simply a biological, psychological, or social animal, but in which a man is a 'human being', an existence which is something far more exciting than the 'mere existence' of a particular organism. This notion of 'existence' is reserved for those who live as individuals, not biologically but individually in their thought and their values. It is a term specially designed for those who are personally committed, who feel their freedom in despair, which recognize their responsibility for their actions.

The meaning of existence is the significance which, one provides for his own life, through realization of one's personal freedom and autonomy, through passionate commitment, through responsibility and the feelings accompanying freedom and responsibility.

To achieve authentic individual existence is to commit oneself, deliberately and passionately to a way of life. Existence is a continuous confrontation with emergencies, competing desires, situations in which choices must be made. The ultimate meaning of existence is not a priori given, but one's ultimate commitment, the choice not of this or that course of action but of a 'mode of existence within which all more particular choices may be determined.

Reason, that is, the capacity to give reasons and justify our choices, can play no part in this ultimate decision, for here we have the need for 'pure' commitment without appeal to any supporting principles, and therefore without reasons or reason. Choices may be called ultimately irrational, means that we cannot ultimately give reasons for his choices, as all choices are founded on one's fundamental choice; and that ultimate choice is itself unjustifiable.

Because our fundamental criteria are unjustifiable, all our choices, which depend on these criteria for their justification, are also ultimately unjustifiable. Yet, we must choose, must "leap to" a way of life if we are to exist, for the only alternative (apart from suicide or a total retreat to inactivity) is to refuse to acknowledge the absence of ultimate justification (what Sartre later refers to as 'bad faith') or, what is worst, to abstain from choice of existence altogether and simply follow the "crowd". Since our ultimate choices are unjustifiable an unhappy spirit such as Kierkegaard can easily find that the demand for choice becomes a crucifying demand; for the burden of choice is entirely on one's own shoulders, no other support, whether it be from society, from one's religious teachings, or from reason itself can be made responsible for one's decision because no criteria can be used in ultimate decisions. One cannot blame these criteria for the choice that one makes. The incredible responsibility of having no one and no value to which to turn leads Kierkegaard to cite despair as an essential ingredient in freedom of choice to cite guilt as an essential component of responsibility.

Kierkegaard attacking on 'reason' says that reason gives the men the illusion that the choices and therefore responsibility for a system of values is out of their hands. For Kierkegaard, man is essentially the chooser of his own values. Everything lies in the act of choosing, in being subjective (passionate and committed). This freedom of choice is itself the most basic of values, what makes a man a human being or an existent individual and the recognition and use of this freedom is far more important than the object of choice.[12]

Thus, the consequences of human liberty and responsibility is to realize and appreciate the concept of "individual existence" which involves the notions of 'choice', 'individual freedom', & 'responsibility' and with these, the concept of 'commitment', 'despair', and 'guilt'.

CHAPTER XIV

MAN AND GOD

The religious stage is that sphere of life, defined by the conception of the individual in relationship to God. There is no doubt that Kierkegaard personally considered relationship to God, as his chosen mode of existence and the central purpose of his writings as he admits in his 'POINT OF VIEW OF MY WORK AS AN AUTHOR', is to arouse the religious view of life in his readers. "Religious", for Kierkegaard is to be taken in a very restricted sense- to be religious is to be a Christian, but a Christian in Kierkegaard's very special sense. Kierkegaard opines that the very membership in the Christian church is the very anti-thesis of being a Christian. In fact, "it is easier to become a Christian when I am not a Christian than to become a Christian when I am one".

Hegel and Kierkegaard (more subtly Kant) take the Christian conception of existence to be 'highest', but yet Kierkegaard conception of Christianity is diametrically opposed to the rationalist conception. For Kant, Christianity was rationally justified by its necessity for practical reason, and God is a postulate in support of morality. Christ enters into Christianity as a corollary of belief in God, for belief in Christ can be rationally justified only so far as this belief is necessary for morality. For Hegel also, belief in God is rational, but the Hegelian God is of a radically different sort, and the rationality of this belief is defended in a very different way. For Hegel, God is not transcendent as for Kant, but immanent. God for Hegel is that subject which is common to all men, and Christ is the symbol of that 'incarnation', that is, the fact that God or spirit is man; and man is God.

Kierkegaard rejects not only the reinterpretation of the Christian conception of God, Christ, and the incarnation approach to Christianity. God is not immanence-such a concept is 'hypocritical atheism'- but transcendence, in Kant's terms, noumenon (intellectual conception), and essentially unknowable and incomprehensible, God is not only separated from man, but forever unknowable by man. God cannot be an object of knowledge, but simply an object of faith, and here Kierkegaard is in complete agreement with Kant. He also shares some of Hegel's views. For, he insists that God must be viewed as a subject; and therefore, Kant's notion that we must have faith; and also, that God exists; is inappropriate. What is needed is faith in God, for the question of His existence once one is within the religious viewpoint, cannot be intelligibly raised.

The central tenet of Christianity is the historical existence of God in the form of man. Hegel is typical of such attempts in his interpretation of Christ as a symbol for the doctrine of the immanence of God. Kierkegaard, however, complains that such imposed plausibility is the destruction of the very doctrine to be rescued. The notion of God as man is not that sort of paradox which can be resolved through the mediation of the Hegelian dialect.

Christianity is not a set of doctrine, but a way of life, a set of values. The absurd doctrines of the incarnations, the trinity, and so on are not important in themselves. It is the attitude of the religious towards these that is important. The appropriate attitude for Kierkegaard is fear, dread, and even terror, before an almighty yet unknowable God, despair and suffering at one's personal weaknesses, and overpowering guilt in the face of sin before God because of these weaknesses. Yet, Christianity is also the love of this god, confidence in his goodness and justice, as well as the fear and despair of Him.[13]

Kierkegaard turns away from external to the inward self, where he meets God through conscience. For by the fact that he turns towards himself and then he turns toward God, and it is a well-established ceremonial convention that if the finite spirit would see God it must begin by being guilty. "In turning toward, himself he discovers guilt".[14]

Kierkegaard sees man and God in utter contrast, separated completely by the gulf of the absurd; yet there must be at least a spark of the divine in man to make him want to risk the jump into the abyss. His emphasis on the irrational paradox also excludes reason completely and his constant demand for despair, despite all its positive aspects, too little attention to the gospels as good news, to the significance of joy.[15]

Kierkegaard writes that "in spite of the fact that I am very far from understanding myself, I have revered the unknown God". The religious understanding of myself has deserted me, I feel like an insect with which children are playing, so pitilessly does existence handle me.[16]

Kierkegaard's faith is the most absolute fideism (faithfulness), we cannot prove any existence, and that of God, least of all; God is not an idea to be proved, but a being in relation to whom we live. "We must not attempt to prove the idea of god, for if it is a blasphemy (profane speaking) to set about to prove his existence to him under his very nose". It is a blasphemy too, to attempt to prove the divinity of Christ by history, which in fact, can teach us nothing about him, because, speaking absolutely, we can know nothing of Christ. He is the paradoxical object of faith; he only exists for faith; to make Christianity seem probable....... That is the destruction of Christianity".[17]

To sum up, it can be said that Kierkegaard has characterized man as a synthesis of the finite and infinite, of the temporal and the eternal, of freedom and necessity. Man shares his humanity with others and forms his ideals and standards.

Man makes choices; in making choices he uses the inwardness of his personality. He cultivates the infinite characteristics and grows into a full human being.

Kierkegaard opines that every existent individual has a passion for freedom. In making choices he passes from one stage to another stage of enlightenment. Man chooses to live an ethico-religious life.

According to Kierkegaard's the true authentic human being is one who recognize the ultimate value of freedom, choice and passion.

Kierkegaard has emphasized the need of responsibility; for him, man is responsible for his actions. Apart from being responsible to himself, man is responsible to his fellow beings too. Since he is the theistic philosopher, he holds man responsible to God through bonds of commitment. He opines that man has inward relationship with God and that is why he practices the ethico-religious mode of living. His religious thought of authentic existence makes man responsible to God to a great deal.

HUMAN LIBERTY AND RESPONSIBILITY IN KARL JASPER'S PHILOSOPHY

CHAPTER XV

KARL JASPERS (1883-1969): Brief Sketch

KARL JASPERS (1883-1969)
Jaspers in 1946

Born

Karl Theodor Jaspers, 23 February 1883, Oldenburg, German Empire

Died

26 February 1969 (aged 86), Basel, Switzerland

Education

University of Heidelberg, (MD, 1908)

Era

20th-century philosophy

Region

Western philosophy

School

Neo-Kantianism (early)[1], Existentialism (late), Existential phenomenology[2] (late)

Main interests

Psychiatry, theology, philosophy of history

Notable ideas

Axial Age; coining the term *Existenzphilosophie*; *Dasein* and *Existenz* as the two states of being,

subject–object split (*Subjekt-Objekt-Spaltung* [de]); theory of communicative transcendence, limit situation[1]

Influences Meister Eckhart, Nicolaus Cusanus, Spinoza, Immanuel Kant, Georg Wilhelm Friedrich

Hegel, Max Weber, Søren Kierkegaard, Friedrich Nietzsche, Martin Heidegger[3]

Influenced Hannah Arendt, Heinrich Blücher, Paul Ricoeur,[1]Hans-Georg Gadamer,[1]

William A. Earle

Courtesy -Wikipedia

KARL JASPERS

Karl Jaspers was born in 1883 at Alden burg, the son of a Bank Manager. As a young youth, he studied law at Heidelberg and Munich, before devoting himself during the next five years to the study of medicine, at Berlin as scientific assistant in the psychiatric clinic in Heidelberg before the First World War in 1914. He was appointed to the chair of philosophy at Heidelberg in 1921, after five years' being on teaching on the staff, he was dismissed for political reasons by the national Socialistic government in 1937, and reinstated in 1948 he was appointed as professor of philosophy at Basel.

CHAPTER XVI

INFLUENCE OF OTHER PHILOSOPHERS ON KARL JASPERS (1883-1969)

Karl Jaspers is a professional philosopher inheriting and participating in the philosophia perennis 'around which all philosophers circle', and at the same time" he is profoundly influenced by Kierkegaard and Nietzsche. Jaspers treats them as the great exceptions. Although Jaspers is not a disciple, he has profited by their intuitions and applied them to the business of philosophy, in the spirit of a true philosopher reflecting upon his own effort to live and living in the light of his reflections.

Philosophy, Jaspers feels, cannot be the same after Kierkegaard and Nietzsche because they have awakened us to our human condition. Kierkegaard is a challenge to our assumptions about us as person. Kierkegaard and Nietzsche have raised the question, what it means to be a human being; and what does it mean to be a Christian, or not too be a Christian?

Karl jaspers translated the reflections of Kierkegaard into more intellectual terms.

We may consider the philosophy of Jaspers as a sort of secularization and generalization of the philosophy of Kierkegaard. Karl Jaspers, like Kierkegaard, is a theist and to a larger extent a religious but he is not a Christian. That is why in the philosophy of Jaspers we are no longer referred to Jesus; but rather to a background of our existence. Humanity has multiple possibilities. But as we develop one, we sacrifice another, and we never attain to that absolute which Hegel prided himself on being able to reach through the unwinding of the idea to its necessary conclusion. The absolute, in Jaspers' philosophy, is "something hidden", revealing itself in fugitive fragments, in scattered flashes like intermittent strokes of lightening.

Philosophy cannot again pretend to be universal knowledge; we have lost our naivety; for we recognize the discontinuities in the realm of being, which the old systems took as one and treated as the object of the universal knowledge, answerable to the structure of thought. The modern starting point, and the strength of our position is in the recognition of this discontinuity between the three forms of being; being there, being oneself, being-in-itself, these forms of being are explored by different methods.

The philosopher living his life participates in all three, philosophy must make and keep the separation and develop the methods of exploration appropriate to each.[1]

We know that being which is something real; we derive our reality from it; yet we cannot interpret it, and as existents we cannot even express ourselves completely. But in this awareness of defeat, which comes most vividly to us in situations in which we are strained to the utmost, we fully realize ourselves whether it be a human drama or in scientific discovery, we sense that there is something other than ourselves, something which exceeds us; and we assert ourselves in our existence by our relation with this transcendence. In this respect we find in Kierkegaard and jaspers the same connections between existence and transcendence.

Jaspers senses deeply those values which escape language, Science and objectivity; and the antithesis resident in our experience of transcendence. He also endeavours to complement the Kierkegaardian and Nietzscheian intuitions with the profound feeling of human communication and human historicity. Communication, and a mutual love with other persons, is at the core of his system.[2]

In the context of existential freedom, the Kantian back ground can be seen in Jasper's philosophy. Jaspers statement that he ascertained the faith by which he lives "guided by the Bible and by Kant", is a remarkably telling index of his attitude towards Kant. Seldom has any philosopher been so strongly influenced by another. Jaspers lists Kant's tautologies, vicious circles, and contradictions, and even tells us that "all sort of statements can be found in Kant".[3]

Thus, we see that Karl Jaspers, who seems to be deeply influenced by the intuitions of Kierkegaard and Nietzsche, has always tried to establish his own identity without following them much. Kant too, left his influences on him. And we can clearly note Kant's influence in Jaspers' philosophical works.

CHAPTER XVII

METHOD OF THINKING

Karl Jaspers, in his philosophical works, to a greater extent follows objective method of study. He opines that scientific interpretation of objects and objective knowledge leads to better solutions of the problems.

Karl Jaspers starts with the assumption that there is a given external world in which the thinker has foothold, a world of stable objects which compels and controls the adherence of knowledge. This world of science is one in which everything known is an object (in the sense that it is experienced as stable and registered in a communicable representation), and is objective (in the sense that what is known about it is universally intelligible and accepted).

This objective knowledge of what is there (being-there) is assumed by many to be the whole ambition of human thoughts; because it is assumed that there is nothing which is not given is stable objects recorded in the human mind in representations which in logical order are universally intelligible and communicable.

This objective certainty which maintains itself; without concurrence; and before which every form of subjectivity has no standing; and is dissolved. The quest for certainty is supported by the fear of liberty; for the anxieties and risk of personal responsibility and decision are escaped if all can be reused to a necessary and universal objectivity; liberty and choice imply the perfection of knowledge uncertainty. Descartes, on the threshold of modern philosophy, enunciating his cogito, announced himself as an individual thinker looking out upon the world from his necessary solitude, an existentialist, but went on to refuse to take the risks inseparable from his recognized position.

His pronouncement turned out to be merely recourse of method, not a personal recognition of the possibility of despair, and the reality of liberty.

Science is incapable in principle of achieving this ideal of objectivity. If it were realized, the world would be exhaustively intelligible to human consciousness as such. But there are vital forms of consciousness lying.

The more or less obscure and fugitive sensations, perceptions, feelings, intuitions, intimations of the private consciousness, which are in part the raw material of public knowledge and in part are intractable to scientific method and responsive to unpredictable manifestation of reality, and the uniquely personal self-determination of the free personality.

Further, inductive knowledge can never be more than probable and in some fields must remain indefinite. It cannot have either a beginning or an end. It is impossible to form out of scientific concepts a coherent image of the world. It has never been successfully maintained that the world is at bottom number, or matter, or spirit, or energy, or any other comprehensive idea borrowed from any of the sciences studying a coherent body of phenomena. There is an irreducible difference between the Science of nature and of man. The sciences of man, of which history is a type are meaningless, a dust of unrelated facts, unless they are more than Sciences, for they require a comprehension of ideas, an appreciation of ethos and reconstruction.

The hope of complete objectivity is linked to the hope of utopia, a final victory over man's practical problems. Both are illusory; both imply the hope of reducing all things to mechanics and manufacture. Neither the world nor knowledge is a unity. There is no refuge from the hazards of real life in such illusions.

Science, then, achieves the clarity and universality of objective knowledge but cannot attain the unity and totality to which reasons aspires. The sciences are empirical and must work as best they can. It is not for the philosophers to give them rules nor practical limits. The limits which he defines are ultimate principles what they can achieve in their own fields is always open and indefinite. Sciences which understand itself and recognizes its ultimate limits is itself philosophy because it is animated by the same spirit the will to know, the persistent attempt to think clearly, the quest for reality etc.

Science is therefore, the necessary ground and first stage of philosophy, but is not capable of achieving the unity and totality which reason cannot renounce. Science is concerned with determinate being and the philosopher beginning with science comes up against its limits, recognizes that he can neither think of absolute being nor renounce the will to think it. He is forced to reflect. According to Karl Japers, philosophy beings with the philosopher's existence, with what he is, not with what he knows; he achieves and communicates not knowledge but himself. The unity and totality which philosophy recognizes, belong to the world in its transcendence (being-in-itself), to which the thinker has access only by means of his own transcendence (being-oneself) of the empirical worlds (being-there). The thinker participates in all three realms of being i.e. (1) Being-in-itself, (2) Being-oneself, (3) Being- there and by that means alone can approach the unity and totality to which his reasons aspire, never by trying to reduce everything to universally intelligible order of being-there. Nothing is more philosophical than science when it abjures metaphysics and is faithful in attention to its own empirical pursuits, for in its docility and persistence; it is then near the authentic reality to which it aspires. But to say this is to shift the accent from science to the scientific worker, who is himself the authentic philosopher where he is going about his own business with understanding and purpose.[4]

Thus, we see that philosophy begins with science and cannot do without it, because there is no other world independent of the objective world which science explores, only one who has passionately given himself up to the exploration of the world can find access to philosophy.

CHAPTER XVIII

NATURE OF MAN

Karl Jaspers thought on nature of man, like Kierkegaard, can be stated briefly, taking into account the finite and indefinite characteristics of man. It can be seen how finite self attains infinite and is different from it.

Man is sure of being not just a natural and historical product. Man is more than that he can know himself. Karl Jaspers treats man as analyzable on three levels. **First,** he is simply an empirical existent. Base in (human being) something which lives in space and time, a thing among other things. **Second,** he is consciousness, the abstract understanding by which he comprehends essential connections among eternal truths. **Third,** he is a spirit (Geist) that aspect which strives to embrace all of his experience, lie, and culture within certain ideal totalities.

Each individual is in his inwardness, as he is to himself as just this unique historical self, is existence. Existence is only a possibility for human nature. Things in the world have no such possibility. This is not, of course, to deny that things exist, but rather to signalize that they exist in a way radically different from authentic existence.[5]

Man, not only exists but knows that he exists. In full awareness he studies his world and changes it to suit his purposes. He has learned how to interfere with 'natural causation'. He is not merely cognizable as existent, but he freely decides what shall exist. Man is mind, and the situation of man as man is a mental situation.

Man is always something more than what he knows of himself. He is not what he is simply once for all, but is a process. He is not merely an existent life, but is, within that life, endowed with possibilities through the freedom he possesses to make of himself.

Man is not finished product which repeats itself from generation to generation, nor is he is manifest life which plainly reveals itself to him. He is dependent upon his own activity, whereby the process of his life is carried on towards an unknown goal. Consequently, there is a profound cleavage in man's innermost nature.

Now coming to man's finite and infinite nature, it is obvious that man's finiteness is first of all the finiteness of all living things. He is dependent upon his environment, upon nourishment and sensory contents; he is inexorably exposed to the mute and blind natural process; he must die.

Man's finiteness is, secondly, his dependence on other man, and on the historical world produced by men collectively. He can rely on nothing in this world.

Man's finiteness lies, thirdly, in the nature of his cognition, in his dependence on the experience that is given him, especially on direct perception.

Man becomes conscious of his finiteness by comparison with something that is not finite, that is infinite.

The infinite becomes actuality for him in his decision, the fulfillment of which directs him to an origin other than that which science makes intelligible to him, his finite existence.

The infinite becomes touched, though not apprehended, first in the idea of infinity, then in the conception of a divine knowledge essentially different from man's finite knowledge, finally in thoughts of immortality. The finite which though unfathomable does enter into man's consciousness causes man to transcend his finiteness by becoming aware of it.[6]

Summarizing, the nature of man, we can thus say that man is more than that he can know himself. According to Jaspers, all living things are finite in nature. Men live for a certain period of time and they must die after that. During their stay in this world, men depend on others rather co-exist with them and develop their personality. Finally, men compare their existence with something which is not finite. When they become aware of it; they aspire to attain this infinite nature and they succeed in achieving this goal, while existing in this very world. The infinite nature which men thus attain is immoral and transcendental in nature.

Karl Jaspers views are different from Kierkegaard, only on the regard that Jaspers has not spoken of a synthesis of finite and infinite nature of man. In Kierkegaard's opinion man is incomplete without this synthesis, but Jaspers makes man to move from his finite existence. Man is complete in both the stages separately and only, the quest for having divine knowledge and a sense of immortality moves him from infinite-to-infinite existence.

Thus, we see that Karl Jaspers to a great extent follows the Kierkegaard in this regard, but maintains his identity.

CHAPTER XIX

HUMAN LIBERTY

Philosophers as well as Scientists are prone to suppose that when we approach to a topic such as freedom, we should first arrive at a definition of freedom. Let us examine a few traditional concepts of freedom to understand freedom as understood by jaspers. The multiple meaning of freedom and necessity lead to contradictory expressions when we try to formulate their existential import.

Freedom is the objective freedom of action as opposed to coercion by physical chains, by psychological threats or blackmail or by physical torture. Freedom is subjective, freedom of action as opposed to the constraints of a given particular situations. Freedom is due to the free determination of the will as put forward by the determinists.

But here, we mean something fundamentally different. The freedom we mean cannot be proved as a reality in the world even though it is the part of man that changes his world and himself. It is perceptible in its effects, not in itself. Philosophically freedom can be made appreciable as Kant put it, but it is not an object of cognition. The difference is our use of the word freedom is as vast as that between objectiveness and non-objectiveness. On the one hand, we use freedom to conceive worldly realities and on the other hand, we use it to transcend these realities to the existence of self being.

Freedom needs its antithesis, if we hear that 'God alone is free, not man', we ought to answer that God's freedom makes no sense unless he is conceived by man. The truth is rather, that man alone can be free as he works his way out of bonds that endure.

Freedom is an existential experience, not an observable one. We have an experience altogether different from the objective one the experience of our freedom.[7] The question of freedom originates in the self who wills its existence. Consciousness of freedom is not a matter of inference but of experience, and arguments for freedom do not prove but rather affirm and assure. Freedom is not known and cannot by any means be thought of as an object remains the alpha and omega of its elucidations. *

It is an agreed fact that freedom is nothing but a choice. For making a choice one must be free or at least feel free to make a choice. And for making choice man must have knowledge. In absence of knowledge there can be no choice and restricted knowledge means limited choice.

From moral view point, at moral level, I am free. To be morally free means to preserve autonomy at all costs, and to do what I see to be right in my own unique situation. It means to accept only those norms which I find to be self-evident because they issue from my innermost self.

Choice is not the resultant of a conflict of motives, not the product of a rational calculus (hedonic or otherwise), and not automatic obedience to law. It is an expression of my own innermost self-assertiveness.[8]

Freedom is the essence of existence. Man in this very world is offered with a choice which he exclusively, makes use of living with other selves. Man exists in this world, always conscious of freedom which is nothing but an idea or intellect which helps in making right decisions. Man, always tries to improve upon his finite nature and catch hold of infinite existence by using his freedom. **

I exist in liberty by conscious separation from my empirical self-adopt all that which is uniquely mine 'as the manifested body of what I can be'. I identified myself with myself and acknowledge the vital impulses of the body. The brute facts of nature, the obligation of duty, the limitations of my situation and of all chosen ends; these enter into my decisions and finally I make an effort for the self-realization. And thus, very self-realization brings about the self-transcendence.

Summarizing, it can be said that although I do not have intrinsic nature but my situation is determined and my authentic choice is necessary. I come to myself as if I were a gift to myself, and I recognize that I have to realize my liberty in the world and to lose it in the transcendence which is its ground and its limit, its source and its goal.

---

* Quoting Karl Jaspers, in "AN INTRODUCTION TO HIS PHILOSOPHY" Wallraft Charles F, says that "I am sure of my freedom, not through thinking but through existing, not through observing and questioning....... but through achieving. "But still there are signs by which existence can hope to recognize the presence of freedom. (Karl Jaspers: AN INTRODUCTION TO HIS PHILOSOPHY-Wallraft Charles F P.112).

** Quoting Karl Jaspers, in "SIX EXISTENTIALIST THINKERS", H.J. Blackham writes that "it is only through freedom that I become certain of transcendence. By freedom, to be sure, I attain to a point of independence from the world, but precisely through the consciousness of my radical attachment to transcendence. P.48)

CHAPTER XX

HUMAN RESPONSIBILITY

Karl Jaspers has heavily stressed the theme of responsibility to oneself and for others. In his "PHILOSOPHIE" he writes that "in communication I sense a responsibility not only for myself but also for the other self".[9]

At another place in "MAN IN THE MODERN AGE", he confesses that man has become what he is, thanks to the tradition which enables him to look back into the obscurity of his beginnings and make him responsible for his own future and that of his associate.[10]

Jaspers says that man must live a life of freedom in the world. He should participate in the struggle of life, all the while bearing himself the responsibility for his own moral decisions and actions. He should partake of the suffering which his life holds out for him, all the while being consciously aware of his own freedom in the world. *

Jasper's interpretation of responsibility**of the individual can best be understood from the following passage, "Man today seeks after freedom, prizing it under both forms" (1) As the liberation of the inner self and (2) As the rule of law in organized society.

But freedom has to be won and maintained in face of the three great tendencies of time. We must be able to make these our servants or they will show themselves masters. The first tendency is socialism. Our mass society, particularly as it has been affected by two world wars, cries out for large-scale organizations and economic planning. We are therefore tempted to push this too far, to make it total. But that is incompatible with freedom. Planning must be kept within definite limits and confirmed t goods of lower order. Jaspers would wish, for example, to retain the free market. We must not worship applied science as though it can solve all our problems. For man in the last resort lives by much that can only be given to him and can never be organized and administered.

The second tendency is towards world unity. Such unity is inevitable. Wars, there may be in the future but they will be in the nature of civil wars, disintegrating the world unity. The question that remains is whether unity will take the form of world empire or world order. To achieve this, we should learn to live in mutual understanding. For this, there have to be a surrender of sovereignty at least to the extent of bringing into being a center of power that will permit to member states the exercise of certain functions, while reserving the rest to itself.

There is, however, a third need, the greatest of all. It is for a faith that will counter the nihilism and unbelief already spoken of. We recognize some of the features of our time in the spectacle of ancient Rome in its decay. What is lacking from the contemporary pictures is anything so virile and so promising as early Christianity was. Clearly, the faith that is to hearten and unite us can be no manufactured product. We need only the rebirth of religion of the Bible in a form appropriate to our time and its needs. It will be faith in God, bringing to conviction that they are not along in face of circumstances not at the mercy of their own impulses, but that there is a power that supports there to. It will be faith in man, so that even an age haunted by the nightmare horrors of Buchenwald will be capable of toleration and the recognition of another as of equal worth with oneself, it will be faith in the possibilities of the future so that our action in this stubborn, yet inviting world.

So, all; turn in the end upon the responsibility of the individual only. He who sees that this is so today will interpret History as Jaspers does for the crux of that interpretation is the recognition of the hour in the past at which the individual awoke to his responsibility as the axis on which all History turn. There are not forces of good that bear us forward to our salvation while we remain passive. But if our problems can be solved only by action, we must not forget that action can only be fruitful in the measure in which it is guided by thought. And for both thought and action there is a further guide in faith that man was made in the image of God and that he is one amid all his decisions, and that is not without a purpose that he is on the earth. Summarizing, Karl Jaspers views on responsibility; we see that Karl Jaspers holds man responsible for himself and for others too. Man is responsible for his actions. Since he co-exists with the other persons, his actions and thereof the responsibility is the concern for others. Man has to act rather perform his actions in such a way that others actions and not thwarted. Other persons should also be free to perform their actions and be responsible for it; not only for themselves but to me also.

Men are conscious of their freedom when they recognize imperatives addressed to them. It is up to them whether they carry them out or evade them. Man cannot seriously deny that they make a decision, by which they decide concerning themselves and that they are responsible. Kierkegaard on the other hand apart from holding man responsible for himself and for others too, has also emphasized the need for man to be responsible to God also. Kierkegaard opines that man through his inward relationship with God, acquired through faith, can attain a high sense of responsibility. Since Kierkegaard's views on human existence are too ethical and religious, this makes him to live throughout an ethico-religious life. And that is why Kierkegaard held himself responsible to God.

Karl Jaspers, though a theistic existentialist himself, is not in agreement with Kierkegaard on making man responsible to God though Jaspers has maintained an ethico-religious concept of human freedom. Bu to a great deal Karl Jaspers has followed Kierkegaard in making man responsible to himself and to others.

---

*Karl Jaspers confesses in; "THE ILLUMINATION OF EXISTENCE" that I am responsible for myself and only in being free, do I discover who I am ..(Karl Jaspers, the illumination of existence, P. 197).

**Karl Jaspers in "PHILOSOPHICAL FAITH AND REVELATION" writes that "where there is a freedom there is a responsibility" (Philosophical faith & Revelation, Karl Jaspers, Tr. E.B. Ashton, P.236).

CHAPTER XXI

INTER-RELATIONS OF PEOPLE

Karl Jaspers' thought on inter-relations of people need special attention. Man attains his freedom in this very world. He has to think of freeing himself from solitude and in doing so man enters into ties with others. Thus, men get inter-related to each other and live harmoniously realizing their freedom and responsibility.

Since man is a social being, he cannot afford to live alone. He is always in the need of others. A man, who, for some or other reasons; tries to live alone is nothing but a half man. He has to accept co-existence to attain the fullness in him.

The nobility, sympathy and loyalty are the true characteristics of a man. And these characteristics are to be shared with others, because the true nobility, sympathy and loyalty cannot be found in an isolated being. It exists in the inter-linkage of independent human beings. Such human beings are aware of their duty to discover one another, to help one another, and to be ever ready for communication. Though they have entered into no formal agreement, they hold together with a loyalty which is stronger than any formal agreement could give. This solidarity extends even to an enemy when self-hood comes into genuine opposition with selfhood.

Men live in society and living there they exist as masses and encounter one another as masses and deduce their rights from mass-power, the self-existent is certainly more assured in its personal trust worthiness. And this very trust worthiness has to be shown rather reflected by one and very other existing individual.

Living together as masses in the society, they enter into close proximity with one another, only by the intimacy of their communication.

The self always requires and seeks communication with other-selves. My uniqueness is elicited and requires the uniqueness of others, and is otherwise unthinkable. Being one-self is not real without manifesting itself in choice. My liberty posits and requires the liberty of everybody else. The formula is; "I will that each other shall be what I strive to become, that he be himself in sincerity and in truth". This appeal to the other is accompanied by self-revelation without reserve.[11]

The formalities, conventions and reserves of ordinary inter-course are inappropriate to communication at the level of being-oneself. One becomes oneself and brings the other to himself in thus opening oneself to him. For this communication is not the sharing of what is in common but insistence upon the differences of each. The beings recognize themselves as united but have as a condition of their reality to assert and maintain their difference and to question and challenge themselves and each other. The truth of each is the truth of himself and for him there is no alternative. It is uniqueness, is a vital assimilation which is his alone; there is no other truth, but there is the truth of others.

Communication is between persons who participates in a common world order and collaborate in common tasks which humanize relation between individuals but communication does not reside in this intercourse, it springs from it. The other is properly constituted for me as a person by my being fully myself, that is, communication is in the world of being, oneself otherwise, he; is another one like me and all others an object and a means, a figure in the world.[12]

Summarizing, I can say that man co-exists in society sharing their nobility, sympathy and loyalty, they share it for their better living. For achieving this they have to enter into communication with one another. And finally, they humanize their relations. Thus, their relations become stronger and stronger. And, in the context of inter-relations of people, it can be boldly said that communication is the most essential of existential tasks the most precious and the most fragile of all possible achievements.

HUMAN LIBERTY AND RESPONSIBILITY IN GABRIEL MARCEL'S PHILOSOPHY

CHAPTER XXII

GABRIEL MARCEL (1889-1969): Brief Sketch and Introduction

GABRIEL MARCEL (1889-1969)

Gabriel Marcel

Born

Gabriel Honoré Marcel, 7 December 1889, Paris, France

Died

8 October 1973 (aged 83), Paris, France

Alma mater

University of Paris

Notable work

The Mystery of Being (1951)

Era

20th-century philosophy

Region

Western philosophy
School

- Christian existentialism, Existential phenomenology[1], Personalism

Main interests

- Ontology, subjectivity, ethics

Notable ideas
"The Other" (*autrui*), concrete philosophy (*philosophieconcrète*), being vs. having as opposing ways of defining the human person
Influences

  - Nikolai Berdyaev, Henri Bergson, Martin Buber, Martin Heidegger, Edmund Husserl[2], Søren Kierkegaard[3]
  - François Mauriac, Josiah Royce[4], Friedrich Schelling

Influenced

  - Pierre Boutang, Emmanuel Levinas, Walker Percy, Jean Wahl, Paul Ricœur, John Paul II

Courtesy -Wikipedia

GABRIEL MARCEL

Gabriel Marcel was born in 1889 into a cultivated family, his father being France minister in Stockholm and afterwards, Director of one or another of the great national collections. His mother died when he was four, and he was brought up by an aunt. The image of his mother (a radiant personality) and the dominion of his aunt (an austere agnostic) inculcated a tension of which he has said, 'the hidden polarity between the seen and the unseen has played a far greater part in my life and thought than any other influence which may be apparent in my writings'. During the first world war, he was not fit for active service and was engaged for the red cross in tracing the missing, an experience which brought home to him the world of differences between the third person and the second. From youth he engaged in dramatic writing (he has published more than 15 pieces) and in philosophical studies, beginning with the idealism of German, English and American thinkers. Musical composition of improvisation, interest him so much that he has taught intermittently since 1912. He was baptized into Roman church in 1929 at the age of 39. He died in 1969.

INTRODUCTION

Gabriel Marcel is a Roman Catholic. He denies having a philosophy that belongs exclusively to him, and which can be put into cut and dried form. Marcel's philosophy is a philosophy of second thoughts, a reflection upon reflection, not raising reflection to a higher degree of abstraction but using reflection to restore concreteness, the unity of living and thinking.

The concern of his philosophy is to restore and explore the truthful and vital experiences which spring from man and world in the completeness of their being and responsiveness of their encounter.[1]

It is customary to count Marcel among the big four of contemporary existentialists, ranging him along with JP Sartre, Martin Heidegger, and Karl jaspers. In general, this is a sound judgment, since he does share many problems and methods in common with these other existentialist philosophers. They all agree that the crucial questions today concern the human individual and the meanings he freely proposes for his relationship with nature, society, and any transcendent values. They view man as a center of freedom which realizes itself in definite acts of interpretation or assignments of meaning, and to examine these acts within their natural and social matrix, the existentialists have to devise some new methods of enquiry.

On most of the issues, which existentialism faces, Marcel is in broad agreement with the other existentialists. Yet it is also a fact that, upon occasions he has repudiated the name" Existentialist" and called himself rather a "Christian-Socratic". This move is intended primarily to differentiate his standpoint from Sartre's, but it also helps to set him off from the other existentialists.

Marcel described his quest for self-understanding as a religious and Christian sort of Socratism. He suggests that the time has come when we have to reconsider the separatism of religion and philosophy. Granting their difference in method and purpose, they nevertheless draw common nourishment from our awareness of participating in being and show a common concern for our use of freedom in regard to our fellowmen and God. Marcel does not advocate any identification between the philosophical act of reflection and the religious act of worship. But he does feel the need to explore more fully their points of relationship.

Alone among the existentialists, Marcel also accepts the Christian faith and regards it as a spur rather than a deterrent to his philosophical work. It makes him more sensitive, rather than less, to the great human problems of evil, social responsibility and freedom.[2]

With regard to Gabriel Marcel's views on problem and mystery, following paragraphwill prove its worth.

Philosophy helps man in discerning those aspects of problems within the public domain, which lead man to know the meaning of human freedom and responsibility. Human existence in the present context can very well be studied problematically in the form of being who encounters the problem and the mystery in this world.

In Marcel's graphic phrase, A mystery is nothing more than a problem which invades the very being of the enquirer and exposes its precarious condition.[3]*

CHAPTER XXIII

NATURE OF MAN

Gabriel Marcel's views on the nature of man rather natures of human existence are not different from other existentialists. Marcel develops his conception of human nature in close agreement with Kierkegaard's theistic conception of nature of man. Kierkegaard and Marcel, conceive of human existence not merely as temporal and finite, but as capable of becoming immortal and eternal in relation to God. They also emphasize that attaining an eternal and immortal state of being in relation to God, is the ultimate spiritual purpose of existence.

Here, comparing Marcel with Heidegger and Sartre, it can be said that Heidegger and Sartre too, like Marcel, believe in the man's finite existence and thereafter attaining the transcendent state of spiritual existence which is not only blissful but also ultimately purposeful.

It can thus be said that Marcel along with Kierkegaard and Heidegger, believe that man in the beginning lie in this world with his temporal and finite nature; but he is not satisfied with his present nature, so in due course of time, he diverts his attention and comes in close relation with God who helps man in changing his nature and thus attaining the immortal and eternal i.e., Infinite nature which is the ultimate purpose of human authentic existence.

---

*Marcel in "PHILOSOPHY OF EXISTENCE", interlinking the mystery and problem, writes that "A mystery is a problem which encroaches upon its own data invading them as it were and thereby transcending itself as a simple problem" (The philosophy of existence, Gabriel Marcel, P.8)

CHAPTER XXIV

HUMAN LIBERTY

Gabriel Marcel's views on human liberty will be discussed here. As for the notion of freedom, obviously, freedom means something quite different from depending on whether it is discussed in a political or social context, for example, or in an ethical or metaphysical one. I think we can see that there is a whole set of concrete conditions which we commonly call freedom, without always having a perfectly clear idea of what we mean by this name. In any case it is clear that we have to guard ourselves against the primitive idea that a free man is a completely independent man. This would be a purely an abstract view which has no basis in actual experience.

If we look at what we call a citizen of a free country we notice that he is subjected to all kinds of obligation, taxes, the military, and so forth. These obligations are part of what it seems to be a citizen, and it would be generally agreed that if a man tried to evade them, he could do so only in the name of a false or at least childish notion of freedom. It must be added that a country can remain free only if its citizens live up to their obligations. Thus, it must be acknowledged that Kant was perfectly right to establish an inner connection between "obligation" and "freedom", in opposition to a purely anarchical theory which identifies obligation with constraint.

It is certain that at every level, whether that of relations between individuals or of relations between nations, the notion of freedom or independence appears incompatible with the actual condition of civilized existence. It is mythical but we have to ask ourselves how this ties in with the relationship between truth and self-respect, * and for that I shall have to deal more directly with the very notion of a "free man'.

Marcel, in THE EXISTENTIAAL BACKGROUND OF HUMAN DIGNITY says that, "to begin with we must take note of the significant fact that not one of us can really say "I am free". There is no meaning in the statement that man is free, and there is of course still less in claiming, with Rousseau, that he is born free. There is no more fatal error that which consists in regarding freedom as an attribute. It can be said that it is exactly the opposite. It is far more appropriate to say that every one of us has to make himself into a free man; that within the bounds of the possible he has to take advantage of the structural conditions, which make freedom possible. In other words, freedom is a conquest always partial always precarious, always challenging and we should remind ourselves again that it is in the midst of a situation of captivity that freedom can be born, at first in the shape of aspiration to be free.

To say that the freest man is the one who has the most hope is perhaps above all to indicate that he is the man who has been able to give his existence the richest significance or stake the most on it.

The freest man I also the most fraternal. The fraternal man is linked to his neighbor but in such a way that this tie not only does not fetter him, but frees him from himself. Now what has been tried to show is that this freedom is of primary importance, for each one of us tends to become a prisoner of himself, not only in respect to his material interests, his passion, or simply his prejudices, but still more essentially in the pre-disposition which inclines him to be centered on himself and to view everything, only from his own perspective. The fraternal man, on the contrary, is somehow enriched by everything which enriches his brother, in that communion which exists between his brother and himself.[4]

Now an attempt will be made to throw some light on autonomy and also the thoughts put forward by Marcel on the distinction between autonomy and the freedom.

Autonomy is nothing but a sort of choice which enables man chose either this or that and in making choice man takes note of his personal autonomy and it rests with him whether to break his relation with others or on the contrary to accept and deepen it. And according to which he chooses, he either shut himself in the isolation of egoism and pride, or open himself up to communion with God and man who he can meet in faith and love.

In autonomy, man awakens to his own value, claim his rights, proclaim his independence, and take his destiny into his own hands. Here, Marcel, examining the distinction between autonomy and freedom, writes that "it is essential to note that autonomy is above all the negation of a heteronomy pre-supposed and rejected; I wish to lead my own life that is radical formula of autonomy. It is here that we can see that tension between the same and the other, which is the very pulse of the world of having. We should further recognize. I think, that autonomy bears on any realm which admits of administration, however conceived. It is in fact, implies the idea of a certain sphere of activity, and can be more closely defined when this sphere can be closely circumscribed in space and time. Anything in the nature of interests, whatever the interests are, can be treated with relative ease as a sphere or district with fixed boundaries, and further, I can, to a great extent, treat my own life as capable of being administered by another or by myself.[5]

Summarizing it can be said that Marcel developed his concept of freedom in close agreement with Kierkegaard's theistic concept of freedom. But he did not share Kierkegaard's negative attitude to life, his emphasis on exclusive subjectivity and man's commitment to God as more essential to his authentic existence than his commitment to other man.

Marcel being Christian is in agreement with Kierkegaard and with Jaspers too, on the subject of human freedom, Kierkegaard and Jaspers and Marcel, maintain an ethico-religious conception of human freedom. Marcel along with other existentialists conceives of human freedom as freedom from inauthentic human existence.

Thus, we see that Marcel's views are not so different from other theistic existentialists. Marcel to a greater extent holds the identical views on human freedom. But his views on the subject are different from atheistic existentialists like Heidegger and Sartre whose conception of human freedom is mainly intellectual and ontological respectively. Heidegger's and Sartre's concept of human freedom will be discussed in 6th and 7th chapter.

---

*Gabriel Marcel in "THE EXISTENTIAL BACKGROUND OF HUMAN DIGNITY" asserting the importance of truth in relation to the freedom of man writes that "the man who has betrayed truth and by that one must understand truth can no longer be a free man. The truth is that it is impossible to conceive of freedom without emphasis on a whole congeries of conditions, so complete as to verge on the contrary, which each of us is obliged both to experience and to dominate, without, however, cherishing the hope of being able to do so absolutely, whether with respect to oneself or to circumstances. (The existentialist background of human dignity, Gabriel Marcel, P.152)

CHAPTER XXV

HUMAN RESPONSIBILITY

Like other existentialists, Gabriel Marcel too holds man responsible for his acts. Gabriel Marcel in "THE EXISTENTIALIST REVOLT" writes that only in voluntary engagement can I impart meaning to that series of events which constitute my past. I assume full responsibility for all my past acts in saying to myself. It is I who has acted in this way. I am what I have done.

Marcel, further holds man responsible not only for himself but for others too. For all the actions performed in the past and being performed at present, man is responsible; Marcel in "HOMO VIATOR", further writes that "I claim to be a person in so far as I assume my responsibility for what I do and what I say. But to whom am I responsible, to whom do I acknowledge my responsibility? We must reply that I am conjointly responsible both to myself and to everyone else, and this conjunction is precisely characteristic of an engagement of the person, that it is the proper mark of the person.

In day-to-day life a man must be aware of his responsibility. For all his actions, he has to carry responsibility with himself. He must perform all his actions in a true spirit. If he does so, his actions will be considered as responsible acts.

Marcel in 'THE DECLINE OF WISDOM' writes that 'no technician can do without the virtue of accuracy, in his world inaccuracy is always punished and the punishment is sometimes terrible. Hence the awareness of responsibility he incessantly carried with him.

At the same time this awareness has to be a particularly of subtle kind. It must not invade the foreground of his consciousness but must remain on its outer fringe. A surgeon performing an operation cannot forget his responsibility for a moment, but it must not weigh on him to the point of being an obsession. It is not weighed on him to the point focus or even concentrates his mind but on his task; responsibility is rather the spirit in which his tasks are carried out of the light in which he sees it.

Comparing Marcel's thought on human responsibility with Kierkegaard's and jaspers, it can be said that Marcel, too moves in the footsteps of Kierkegaard and Karl Jaspers. Marcel to a greater extent is in agreement with both of them in this regard. Along with Kierkegaard and Jaspers, Marcel holds man responsible for himself and for his fellowmen or to others.

Marcel, though Christian and to a greater extent theistic existentialist, does not clearly hold his views like Kierkegaard who makes the authentic individual responsible, apart from being responsible towards himself and others, to God. Marcel seems to remain silent on the subject in this domain.

Summarizing, it can be said that, like other theistic existentialists, Marcel holds man responsible to himself and to others. He not only emphasizes that man must be aware of his responsibility, but also that he must perform his acts in a true spirit in order to make it a responsible action. I differ with Soren Kierkegaard only on the regard where he holds man responsible to God for his actions. Man cannot do away like this. As long as Kierkegaard maintains that man is responsible for himself for his actions and to others. I am in agreement with him.

Concluding, I can say that man is responsible for himself for the actions he himself has performed and also to others. Man has to have an awareness of doing things or performing actions responsibly. He must perform all the actions in a true spirit and to be specific with a high degree of sense of responsibility.

CHAPTER XXVI

MAN, AND GOD

Gabriel Marcel, although the obedient churchmen, is never the orthodox theologian. His theology is always a highly personal reflection upon experience. Like Kierkegaard, the theistic existentialist, Gabriel Marcel too believes that the truth of human existence comes to be disclosed only through its commitment and man's inward relationship to God.

Marcel conceives of human existence not merely as temporal and finite, but as capable of becoming immortal and eternal in relation to God. He also emphasizes that the 'inwardness' of man's relation with God can be sustained only by his faith. Marcel further maintains that man can attain an eternal and immortal state of being in relation to God and that this is the ultimate spiritual purpose of authentic existence.

Marcel follows Kierkegaard's example in remaining faithful to the religious or Christian inspiration, namely that man is not really himself, is not really free save in his relation to God. *

Marcel believes that man commitment is not only to God but also to other men and that the two commitments are interrelated. Man's moral relations with others give him a fullness of being which he otherwise lacks and also serves as the medium through which he can enter into relation with God. Man's faith in God, on the other hand sustains and supports in him the cultivation of the spirit of love, fidelity and service towards his fellowmen and a deviation from this path of commitment would land him in treason. In religious terminology, man's commitment to God, is a matter of trust or belief in him which is an expression of his faith in him.

Faith, as Gabriel Marcel conceives it, is not at all a matter of the intellect. It depends essentially on moral dispositions and on an attitude of the will. It consists less in believing something than in trusting someone. It consists rather in fidelity to a person than adherence to a dogmatic formula. **

Faith is not merely believing that God exists but believing in God; as pointed out above, it is not at all a matter of intellectual and propositional affirmation of God but is itself the movement of freedom into bonds of commitment to God. In faith, man trusts Good and believes that he will respond to him and not betray him in adversity.

Marcel further claims that "if I decide to live in faith, hope and charity, cultivating patience and humility in profound dependence upon God. I am playing for a stake which I believe to exist and to be worth the loss of everything else; I am affirming what I am against what I have and my life is the venture I make".[6]

Thus, regarding Marcel's views on man and God, it can be said that human transcendence is not merely horizontal as passing from the present to the future in order of time but is 'vertical' as passing beyond the finite and the temporal to the transcendent and the eternal, and establishes its 'being' in relation to him.

Marcel agrees with Kierkegaard in emphasizing that man has to enter into a personal relationship of commitment to God if he is to live an authentic human existence but man cannot commit himself to God without committing himself to his fellow beings by entering into relations of trust, love and sympathy with them as part of his commitment to God, thus finds special emphasis in the philosophy of Gabriel Marcel.

---

*Gabriel Marcel- in 'METAPHYSICAL JOURNAL' further clears the relationship with God by writing that "there must be no question of enclosing God within the circle of his relation with me". (Gabriel Marcel, Metaphysical Journal, P. 281)

**Marcel, in 'THE EXISTENTIAL BACKGROUND OF HUMAN DIGNITY' says that "faith is not the affirmation of an existence but it is the problem of the existence of God. (Gabriel Marcel, the existential background of human dignity, P.27).

CHAPTER XXVII

INTER-RELATIONS OF PEOPLE

Gabriel Marcel distinguishing himself from the other existentialists by his special emphasis on man's being-with-others as expressing the whole truth of human existence. Marcel draws a distinction between two kinds of persons.

1. The 'unhandy' and 'unavailable'.
2. The 'handy' and 'available'.

The 'unhandy' and 'unavailable' are those who are self-centered and whose existence is 'lost' in the pursuit of their personal desires and pleasures. Because of their selfishness, they are incapable of love, compassion and sacrifices for others and hence 'unhandy' and 'unavailable' for others.

Distinguished from these are the 'handy' and 'available' who transcend the limitations of their petty ego and actively enter into relations of love, sympathy, and service with others, thereby making themselves 'handy' and 'available' for others.[7]

Man is not an 'isolated being', but his being is always discovered in his 'living communication' with others. Man has his structure constituted as being-with-others; and he discovers his freedom only as part of his structure.

Marcel, in "BEING AND HAVING", postulates that 'not only do we have a right to assert that others exist * but I should be inclined to contend that existence can be attributed only t others. I would go so far as to say that it is of the essence of the other that he exists, I cannot think of him as the other without thinking of him as existing. The other, in so far as he is other, only exists for me in so far as I am open to him, in so far as he is a thou; But I am only open to him in so far as I cease to form a circle with myself, inside this circle the other becomes the idea of the ether, and the idea of the other is no longer the other; bit the other is related to me.

Marcel does not believe that human relations are basically disharmonious. Freedom does not consist in a man's self-assertion so as to alienate himself from others and set himself against them; but in freedom man frees himself ego-centricism by participating in the creative life of the community. Man identifies himself with the interests of others and enters into harmonious human relation with them. Man's freedom thus unites him with society and does not alienate him.

Man living in society forms a sort of community and they co-exist together with a sense of harmony among each other. **

This bond of communication is maintained by a common recognition of weakness, but this weakness change in the light of a common destiny. It is on this personal level that true fraternity is possible as distinct from the rational abstract definition of fraternity is not only an anthropomorphism it is through divine fraternity alone that an existing, authentic and effective community can be realized.

Thus, it can be said that men accept the existence of fellow beings. Living together they share together the love sympathy and mutual respect. They form a community and live-in harmony. The good fellows rise above the selfishness, personal desires and pleasures. They always look for the common benefit and pleasures of the community and also for a common destiny.

Man's being with others express the truth, in a real sense of human existence. In real terms they live in a true spirit of friendship, compassion and brotherhood.

---

*Gabriel in "HOMO VIATER", writes that from the same view point, as I pointed out under the heading HUMAN RESPONSIBILITY, i.e. "I tend to establish myself as a person in so far as I assume responsibility for my acts and so behave as a real being". I might also say that I establish myself as a person in so far as I assume responsibility for my acts and so behave as a real being". I might also say that I establish myself as a person in so far as I really believe in the existence of others and allow this belief to influence my conduct. (P.22)

**Gabriel Marcel affirms that a true community is possible only when persons mutually recognize each other as different, and as existing together in their very difference. "What brings me nearer to a being, what binds me effectively to him, is certainly not to know that he could verify and ratify an addition or a division that I could have done on my own. Much rather, it is to appreciate that he (like me) has undergone certain trains, that he is subject to some vicissitudes that he has been loved and that also he has a childhood, that other beings have set their hopes in him; it is also to realize that he is called to suffer, to wither, to die'. (IBID, P.14)

CHAPTER XXVIII

DESPAIR AND DEATH

Gabriel Marcel's views on despair and death may be stated briefly here. The phenomenon of despair and death finds a special emphasis in the philosophy of Kierkegaard, Sartre, Heidegger and Gabriel Marcel. They affirm the inevitability of death and the transistoriness of human existence. They also note with concern that man usually ignores this basic truth of his empirical existence and allows himself to be deceived by the seeming permanence of his existence in the world. This self-delusion is the basis of his inauthentic existence. The 'acceptance' of death as the inevitable prospect of man's present life awakens him from his inauthentic existence and directs him to authentic existence. The phenomenon of death is thus credited with an 'ethical' significance in the philosophy of Kierkegaard, Heidegger, Sartre and Marcel.

Marcel, as a matter of fact, is not without the existentialist anguish, in particular that provoked by the thought of death.

Marcel considers despair as a central datum of meta-physics. Man is capable of despair, capable of hugging death, of hugging his own death.

Marcel, appreciating Kierkegaard, says that, "The essential merit of Kierkegaard and his school, to my mind, is their having brought this datum into full view. And metaphysics ought to take up its position just there, face to face with despair. For the catholic existentialist, despair is no more than a passing inducement; hope is the texture and foundation of life, and is its essential condition. *

According to Kierkegaard, man faces and accepts despair in his ethico-religious stage of existence. Despair discloses to him his isolation and separation from God; hence out of despair he takes an existential leap to faith in God, least he should succumb to sickness unto death. Faith in God is thus a 'life necessity'. In the ethico-religious stage of existence, man commits himself to inward decisions and responsible actions with earnestness and passion and enters into bonds of commitment to God. But man is not able to sustain himself always in God relationship and hence arises his religious suffering which is due to the inevitable moments of separation from God. However, suffering only intensifies his longing for God and leads him into closer bonds with him.

Despair is thus a turning point in man's life from aesthetic to the ethico-religious stage of existence and by accepting and facing despair man chooses to enter upon a life of personal decisions and concrete responsible actions.

Death occupies a central place in Martin Heidegger's exposition of human existence. He can describe this as a being-towards-death. For, Heidegger, death is man's ultimate and 'own most' possibility. It is the 'end' (goal as well as termination) of a man's life whereby man becomes a "whole". For Heidegger, as for Kierkegaard, death permeates all of life, and it is death which forces us to see our 'true' selves. Death limits the life; with the knowledge of death, life becomes more urgent and time becomes more meaningful.

Jean Paul Sartre too, clearly acknowledges the importance of death but denies its value as a goal in living. To be sure, "death haunts me at the very heart of each of my projects as their inevitable reverse side'. For Sartre, Death is only a boundary of human life, and it is not part of my life or part of my future or part of my possibilities at all. Sartre further says, Death is not an obstacle to my projects, since death is always beyond my subjectivity. There is no place for it in my subjectivity.

Summarizing, it may be said that existentialists such as Kierkegaard, Martin Heidegger, Sartre, and Gabriel Marcel believe that present life of man is his only life and that death is the end of it; his possibilities are hence limited to his present life. He has to choose one for all between the authentic and the inauthentic modes of existence in his present life. The awareness of death as the final termination of his present life is the basic condition of his choices between the authentic and the inauthentic existence and makes it most urgent. Even Kierkegaard and Gabriel Marcel, who promise the possibility of an eternal and transcendent status of being to man, do not recognize the possibility of the existence of next life.

---

*Gabriel Marcel in "HOMO VIATER", says that "it is in hope and not in despair, that we rise to authentic existence; I am not far from believing that hope is to the soul what breathing is to the living being. Where hope is lacking; the soul wills and exhausts itself" (Gabriel Marcel, Homo Viater, P. 10)

PART-II

HUMAN LIBERTY AND RESPONSIBILITY IN ATHEISTIC EXISTENTIALISM

HUMAN LIBERTY AND RESPONSIBILITY IN FRIEDRICH WILHELM NIETZSCHE'S PHILOSOPHY

CHAPTER XXIX

FRIEDRICH WILHELM NIETZSCHE (1844-1900): Brief Sketch and Introduction

FRIEDRICH NIETZSCHE (1844-1900) in Basel, Switzerland, c. 1875

Born

Friedrich Wilhelm Nietzsche,15 October 1844, Röcken, Saxony, Prussia

Died

25 August 1900 (aged 55), Weimar, Saxe-Weimar-Eisenach, German Empire

Alma mater

University of Bonn, Leipzig University

Era

19th-century philosophy

Region

Western philosophy,

School

Continental philosophy, Nietzscheanism

Other schools

Anti-foundationalism, Atheism, Dionysianism[1], Dionysian pessimism[2], Existentialism, Immoralism[3], Metaphysical voluntarism, Nihilism / anti-nihilism[4][5], Perspectivism, Philosophical realism[6][7], Political realism[8]

Institutions

University of Basel

Main interests

Aesthetics, classical philology, ethics, metaphysics, ontology, philosophy of history

poetry, psychology, tragedy, truth theory, value theory

Notable ideas

Amor fati, Apollonian and Dionysian, Eternal return, Fact–value distinction, Genealogy

God is dead, Herd instinct, Last man, Master–slave morality, Nietzschean affirmation

Nihilism, Perspectivism, *Ressentiment*, Transvaluation of values, *Tschandala*,*Übermensch*,

Will to power

Influences,

Zoroaster, Homer[9], Hesiod[10], Archilochus[11], Theognis of Megara[12], Milesian School[13], Pindar[14], Heraclitus, Parmenides[13], Aeschylus, Sophocles, Euripides[15], Socrates, Plato, Xenophon, Epicurus[16], Thucydides[17], Diogenes Laërtius[18], Machiavelli[19], Montaigne[20], Shakespeare[21], French MoralistsSpinoza, Kant, Herder[22], Goethe, Hölderlin, Hegel[23], Stendhal, Schopenhauer, Ortlepp, EmersonFeuerbach, Sainte-Beuve[24], Mill, Strauss, Darwin, Herzen[25], Wagner, Burckhardt, Spencer[26]Baudelaire, Dostoyevsky, Maupassant, Renan, Lange[27], Bahnsen[28][29], Teichmüller[27], Spir,Mainländer[30][31], von Hellwald[32], Rée, Bourget[33]

Influenced

Adler[34], Adorno, Auden, Bataille, Blanchot, Brandes, Buber, Campbell, Camus, Castoriadis, Cioran, Deleuze, Derrida, Foucault, Hamsun, Heidegger, Iqbal, Jung, Kaufmann, Klossowski,Sarah Kofman, MacIntyre, Mann, Malraux, Mencken, Nehamas, Proust[35], Rand, Ricœur, Rogers, Sartre, Shestov, Spengler, Steiner, Stevens, Strauss, Strindberg, Tillich, Tönnies, Unamuno, Unger, Weber, Weizmann, Willard, Yeats

Courtesy -Wikipedia

FRIEDRICH NIETZSCHE

Friedrich Wilhelm Nietzsche was born in 1844, near Leipzig in Germany. He was the son of a protestant pastor, who died before the child was five. At school he was influenced by Greek studies and by the poet Holderlin, himself a passionate Grecian. Meant for the church, he abandoned theology for philosophy and followed Ritschel of the University of BONN to that of LEIPZIG, where Goethe had been inscribed a student one hundred years earlier. He took Goethe as his master; fell under the spell of Schopenhauer, German philosopher realizes the Greeks, above all the pre-Socratics, and such modern as Novalis, Brentano, and Heine. During his period of military service an injury to the chest proved troublesome and he was invalidated out. He finished his studies at Leipzig and obtained a chair in philosophy at Basel, where he was a colleague of Jacob Burckhardt. Before he left Leipzig, he had met Wagner there. And at Basel he was within easy reach of their home and formed an enchanted intimacy with Wagner and Cosima. Music had always been a necessity to him. In the next ten years i.e., 1869-1879 his health broke down and he became alienated by Wager's romantic Germanism and mystical Christianity. He has to give up his post. During the following 10 years, i.e., 1879-1889, without country, profession, or home, racked by migrating and moving from place to place (within a year), he wrote the books by which he is known. In the year 1889 mental disorder supervened, and he remained deranged till he died in 1900 at Weimar in the care of his sister.

INTRODUCTION

Atheistic existentialism is usually regarded as beginning with Nietzsche. His contribution to the movement is the theme that "God is dead' and that each individual must seek his own value, providing a bridge to future. That is why perhaps the best starting point for discussing the positive aspect of Nietzsche's thought development is his frequent statement that 'God is dead; we have killed God; God has died'. This is obviously not the statement of a straight-forward atheist. The atheist would simply say that there is no God, that belief in him is a non-sensical superstition and has no foundation whatever. But the phrase 'God is dead' refers to loss of faith in God or religion. Nietzsche recognizes that Christianity has lost its hold over the majority of the Europeans', especially over the majority of intellectuals, and this the most significant event in the nineteenth century. For, as European civilization had been based on the Christian concept of God, the disappearance of faith must necessarily leave a void at the very core of our civilization; instead of God there is nothing. Nietzsche recognizes, too, that this situation is fraught with danger this sense of emptiness is not static, it grows constantly and destructly, undermining more and more convictions. More and more concepts, values, beliefs, creeds hit thereto the foundations of our lives have crumble and have to be discarded. In the end we are confronted with nothingness as the core of our existence. Such a sense of emptiness is still increasing and threatens to engulf everything of real value which is still left to us.1

CHAPTER XXX

OBJECTION TO CHRISTIAN VIEWS

Nietzsche's upbringing as a pastor's son was deeply religious and his gradual disappointment and disillusionment with Christianity came as a result of the deeply imbedded strata of hypocrisy both in Christian dogma and practice.

Against Christianity, Nietzsche repeats the largely justified charge which has been raised in the far East ever since the 13th century; that Christians do not practice what they preach, no matter what their holy books say. As Nietzsche puts it "A Buddhist acts differently from a non-Buddhist; a Christian act like everybody else and practices Christianity of rituals.2

Nietzsche's reaction to 19th century Christianity is as profound as it is extreme. Christianity exploits man's basest desire, first of all, by its appeal to that most dangerous of illusions-equality; and secondly, through its distortion of the individual will-to-power by teaching the Christian that he is one of the God's elect. Thus, to Nietzsche the most dangerous and the most terrible disease of contemporary European's man was Christianity. Nietzsche found things to admire in the person of Jesus, particularly his anarchism, his kindness and his hatred of hypocrisy; but he rejected the essentially passive and negative attitude of Jesus toward earthly life. Nietzsche regarded this as an inversion of the will-to-power, such that it turned inward against itself.

For Nietzsche the ultimate's sin of Jesus was his permitting himself to be overcome by pity, thus becoming the progenitor of the "noble life" which promised the meek the domination of the earth and privileged position in life beyond death.

Nietzsche's attitude to Jesus is particularly characteristic of his ferocious attacks against Christianity directed solely against the church. The church is precisely that against which Jesus preached and against which he thought the disciples to preach.

Christianity came into existence in order to lighten the heart. Christianity crushed and shattered man completely and buried him as though in mud; into a feeling of total depravity, it then suddenly shone a beam of divine mercy, so that, surprised and stupefied by this act of grace, man grave vent to cry of raptures and for a moment believed he bore all heaven within him. If the Christian dogmas of a revengeful God, universal sinfulness, election by divine grace and the danger of everlasting damnation were true, it would be a sign of weak-mindedness and lack of character not to become a priest, apostle or hermit and, in fear and trembling, to work solely on one's own salvation. It would be senseless to lose sight of one's eternal advantage for the sake of temporal comfort.

Nietzsche in the "BEYOND GOOD AND EVIL", discussing morality, classifies morality into two, master morality and slave morality. To Nietzsche, Christianity is a slave morality which extols qualities such as sympathy, kindness and humility. Christian morality is morality of negation, morality of renunciation. Renunciation is denial of the life of instincts, suppression of life, or death of human emotions. Christian morality has done away with the masters, and has redeemed the human race and the 'redemption of the human race', means, vulgarizing mankind. This morality has weakened the human race, and therefore it must be demolished. It must be supplanted by the will-to-power, the will-to-over-power, the will to-war, the will to overthrow the will to become masters.

Weakness, humility, patience and forgiveness must be replaced by strengths, bravery, self-assertion self-aggrandizement, ruthlessness, resolutions, honour and pride.

Further in the "BEYONG GOOD AND EVIL", Nietzsche says, "Christianity which worships meekness and pity, and exalts slave morality is the greatest enemy of mankind and most hostile to the birth of new species. Nietzsche does not believe in God. The Christian faith is a sacrifice; the sacrifices of all freedom, all pride, all self-confidence of spirit, it is at the same time, subjection, self-derision and self-mutilation".3

Nietzsche's views on morality and the distinction between slave and master morality has been subjected to severe criticism. According to Nietzsche Christian morality is morality of negation and renunciation which praises enthusiastically the qualities such as sympathy, kindness, patience. Heidegger and Sartre too emphasize the need of ethical and moral life for man. For both, freedom is basically the ontological truth of human existence and that the practice of this 'truth' in man's authentic existence manifests on his ethical and moral life. For both, Heidegger and Sartre, to be 'true' to one's existence is also to be ethical and moral.

Karl Jaspers too emphasizes the need for leading an ethico-religious life; But Jaspers along with Heidegger and Sartre do not classify morality into slave or master's morality. They seem to remain silent on the subject.

Nietzsche's views on morality are subjected to criticism and forgiveness. He opines that to overcome this one must use will-to-power, in order to attain the master morality.

Firstly, Nietzsche commits a mistake in dividing the morality into slave and master morality. Thus, he discriminates the human race or mankind into two groups i.e., masters and slaves. In this discriminating mankind, he wrongly supposes the qualities for slave are sympathy, kindness, patience and forgiveness and for masters are brave, self-assertiveness, resoluteness having honour and pride etc.

It is not feasible to do away with slaves and have only masters. Both are complementary to each other. Slaves or masters to themselves have no import. Each will perish in absence of the other. One cannot be allotted with certain number of good qualities for all along the life. In due course of time a slave may turn into master or a master may turn into a slave. Likewise, the qualities are not the final property of one group of people i.e., of slaves or of masters, living in society one is free to develop and cultivate the good qualities which are really good from social view point. Both, slave and masters have to co-exist. Slave morality and master morality have to go hand in hand.

Giving Christianity a state of slave morality is a mistake committed by Nietzsche. The qualities which are to be possessed by Christian religion such as sympathy, kindness, patience and forgiveness are of high import. Nietzsche has thought of demolishing the Christianity. Had he thought of making Christianity for that matter of humanity or mankind apart from being sympathetic, kind, having patience and forgiveness, also to be brave, self-asserting, self-aggrandized, resolute, having honour and pride then Nietzsche must have added a feather to his cap but throughout his life he concentrated in doing away with Christianity?

It is a great mistake to hold Christians the enemy of mankind or of whole of human race and hostile to the birth of new species i.e., masters. Men are not born masters they become masters living in this very world.

Summarizing it can be said that Nietzsche's objection to the Christianity is not genuine. We can be in agreement with Nietzsche to the extent that he has lost faith in Christianity for some or other reason, and non-existence of God. It's a matter of one's faith. It does not matter whether God exists or not.

It cannot be disregarded that Nietzsche is an atheist; certainly, it was first time for the movement of existentialism to feel different from the conservative religious thoughts. At last, Nietzsche dared to speak straight in terms of assaulting the religion particularly Christianity, and established his identity as the first aesthetic existentialist.

CHAPTER XXXI

HUMAN EXPERIENCE

Nietzsche was indeed an exceptional character. He had prophetic dreams and apocalyptic experiences round which his thoughts gathered. He knew there was one central experienced reality; a great longing that could never be appeased, a longing for the kingdom, the power and the glory. He fully understood what existentialists mean by 'transcendence', He wrote, "Man is created to be surpassed"'. Man can attain his fullness only by living above himself.

He insisted with all his strength that "man is an evaluating animal and can exist only by selecting moral values to which to cling and by which to live. This is the truth embodied in human experience from the beginning and radiantly expounded by him in all his works.4

Nietzsche, in the "Beyond Good and Evil", writes even in the midst of the most remarkable experiences, we still do just the same; we fabricate the greater part of our experience and can hardly be made to contemplate any event, except as 'inventors' thereof.

He further writes "What we experience in dreams, provided we experience it often, pertains at last just as much to the general belongings of soul as anything" actually" experienced; by virtue, thereof we are richer or poorer, we have a requirement more or less and finally, in broad day light and even in the brightest moments of our dreams. He even says that dreadful experiences raise the question whether he who experiences them is not something dreadful also.

It was Kant's insight that the self cannot be that to which our impressions and ideas have a reference. Impressions and ideas, or experiences are not referred to the self, the self is what makes experiences possible as the synthesizing activity of its elements; otherwise, experiences could never be my experience. The self is neither phenomenon nor thing-in-itself, but rather the transcendental unity of consciousness which must be able to accompany all thinking. The self is not a thing or a substance at all; it is what makes the unity of experience possible, what makes "experience" my experience.

The self is the core of experiencing subject which persists through the multiplicity of what experience.

Nietzsche does not deny any kind of consciousness as a unity as either a naïve or a transcendental unity. He denies that consciousness has absolute substratum (subject) or is the cause of experience. Nietzsche has no universal subjectivity, no universally valid forms of sensibility and categories which structure experiences.

Nietzsche points to a type of human being who experiences differently from the average man. This manner of experiencing is active, not in the sense of arbitrary fabrication but in the sense of being able to experience and shape a higher dimension of reality.

Nietzsche, in the "will-to-power"' writes that "those overpowering artists who let a harmony sound forth from every conflict are those who bestow upon things their own power and self-redemption; they express their innermost experience in the symbolism of every work of art they produce their creativity in gratitude for their existence.

One of the experiences which negated the framework of time for Nietzsche was the experience of timelessness. For him there is no gap in experience. There is continuity between the vital, the psychic and the spiritual planes and Nietzsche found ecstatic satisfaction in communion with nature. Nietzsche gives little importance to the notion of conscience.

Lastly, Nietzsche, for all his understanding of the tragic experiences, refused to be involved in it in the existential sense, feeling all the time like an actor in a play.

CHAPTER XXXII

HUMAN LIBERTY

Nietzsche explicitly denies human freedom and exhibits a genuine if philosophical-distaste for the "concrete worldly existence" of man. Nietzsche is a philosopher of life and of the world. He says "one strives for freedom for the sake of power, not the other way around". Nietzsche considers "will-to-power" and instinct to freedom" to be one and the same drive, and much of what he says of 'power' is identical to what so many philosophers have said about freedom. Therefore, Nietzsche's philosophy of power could be understood in terms of a philosophy of freedom.

Kierkegaard's makes virtually no mention of the "free-will problem"' but simply assumes the reality of the individual freedom he values. His concept of freedom does have a basis in his phenomenological descriptions of our experience of freedom and the actuality of this freedom and the value of it.

With regard to question of free will-Jaspers pointed out that those who argue for "freedom of the will" are usually motivated by a fear that responsible action will cease on the day that all men become determinists. And those who argue against it may be motivated by truthfulness; that is; they acknowledge that they cannot find freedom anywhere in the world. Jasper's freedom of action or choice is also freedom psychologically defined; the freedom of the will itself is not in question, and question concerning whether one's motives or character or constitution are determined, whether one is free to choose the standards by which choices are made, and so forth, are not raised.

Nietzsche harshly disagrees with the current conception of freedom, more often than not denoting civic, moral responsibility as well as autonomy (Kant and Hegel) and associating freedom with the comfortable bourgeois moralities; he most vehemently hates freedom that connotes the passive, the un-striving something that is simply given {as Kant's postulate of freedom}, or something found in conformity and good citizenship {Hegel's positive freedom}. Will-to-power shares neither of these connotations; its forcefulness resides in its connotations of a struggle and fight.

As for freedom as a metaphysical concept, Nietzsche says little of it except to dismiss it as useless; as for the celebrated freewill problem,

Nietzsche dismisses both free-will and determinism as more confusion. He says, in fact, there is no such thing as will and if there is no will, there is no freewill.

While Nietzsche considers it untenable either to accord or to deny "freedom of the will" to human beings, however, he is quite prepared to allow that the notion does have some genuine experiential significance. The question of "freedom of the will" has raised a hot controversy among the philosophers of different ages.

In ordinary usage, the expression, "freedom of the will" means freedom to do what we will to do, without any compulsion for restraint. But here the question is whether we are free to will what we will, and how we come to will it, whether we are free to choose between alternative possibilities i.e., possible lines of action or whether we are compelled to choose one of them by something other than ourselves. In other words, does our willing a line of action depend essentially upon ourselves alone and is therefore autonomous of self-determined? Or does it depend on any other things extraneous to the self and is thus heteronymous or other determined?

Some are advocates of the doctrine of freedom of the will, they are called libertarians and those who deny is called determinists.

According to the doctrine of freewill, in willing we are always conscious of willing freely or determining the course of our actions from within ourselves and for our own good, without being determined by anything antecedent to, or external to, ourselves, and the consciousness of freedom is especially distinct in the process of deliberation and resolution.

Kant argues that freedom of will is a postulate of morality. In moral, judgment there is a sense of "oughtness" or moral obligation; this moral obligation implies freedom of the will, "though oughtest, therefore thou canst "Duty, responsibility, Justice, accountability, merit and demerit, virtue and vice would be quite meaningless if there were no freedom of will. A true and adequate metaphysical theory of the world (objective idealism) confirms the doctrine of free will. According to it the world, the finite spirit, and God are real. The world is the manifestation of the divine power. The finite spirits are finite reproduction of God and as such they share in the freedom or self-determining power of God. The human soul shares in the freedom of God, but the freedom of man is not absolute but relative; it is limited, to a certain extent, by the organism and the physical forces of nature, by his relation to other man, and by the freedom of God.7

The Hindu concept of freedom is based on the assumption of the substantive conception of the transcendent soul. The soul's empirical state of being-in-the-world is regarded as its state of bondage, which is described differently in the different systems; Advaita Vedanta regards it an 'illusory' from the stand point of the transcendent eternal freedom of the soul, which in 'truth' is non-different from Brahman. The Sankhya and the Nyaya-Vaisesika system alienate the empirical state of bondage from the transcendent state of freedom explain this alienation on the basis of their respective kind of dualism. The Vishisht-Advaita and Dvaita Vedanta believe in the temporary reality of the state of bondage and maintain that it does not affect the inherent freedom of the soul.

But though freedom is held to be eternal and is something which can neither be produced nor destroyed, all these systems distinguish between the authentic and the inauthentic modes of human existence. In inauthentic existence the awareness of the soul's freedom is concealed due to a mistaken conception of its true nature, and the way of life intended to restore the soul to the awareness of its freedom through the right knowledge of its 'true nature' is the authentic existence.

The Hindu system of philosophy believes that the process of realizing the freedom of the soul may involve a series of lives; each life being determined by the activity (karma) of the individual in the previous life. It is only by transcending this temporal order of existence that the freedom of the soul can be realized. The Hindu concept of freedom is thus metaphysical and non-temporal as distinguished from the temporal conception of freedom propounded by Heidegger and Sartre and rests on the substantive conception of the eternal and immortal soul.

The Hindu philosophical system agree with the Christian existentialist, Kierkegaard and Marcel in postulating the transcendent and eternal freedom of the souls but unlike the Christian existentialist the Hindu philosophical systems maintain that the soul is not created by God but is co-eternal with him. The emphasis on the doctrine of karma and on transmigration of soul is also a distinctive feature of the Hindu philosophical system.

Nietzsche on the other hand maintains that "man as a spiritual being is self-determinism or free. He determines his own activity. He is not determined by external forces; but is not absolutely free. His freedom has limits. It is limited by his innate endowments, physical and mental makeup, transmitted to him by heredity and by his physical and social environment.

But he can transform even his limits into the means and material of his self-development and self-realization.

The contrast between the great majority of human beings who are incapable of 'becoming free' and those who are capable of doing so (although even they can do so only with difficulty) is one of the main themes of the chapter of the Nietzsche's work, "BEYOND GOOD AND EVIL" entitled "the free spirits". Nietzsche contends, independence is for the very few; "it is a privilege of the strong, and even the strong and reckless, if they attempt it.... Without inner constraint. The self-mastery involved in the achievement of such "inner constraint" is an essential aspect of freedom as he conceived it; and it is with this sort of mastery in mind that he links freedom with struggle and conquest, and characterizes the 'free spirit' in terms of complementary notion of 'independence and command'. He considers freedom rare and true and "free spirit", regarding freedom as a distinctive attainment of exceptional human beings. But it is crucial to observe that for him such human beings. But it is crucial to observe that for him such human beings can and do appear. They constitute at least partial exception to the generalization. Freedom, he suggests should be understood as facility in self-direction and such facility, which he regards as pre-supposing both, 'fortunate organization' and the various forms of self-mastery, is a possibility which may be realized.

Nietzsche's equating "will-to-power" with human freedom deserves a strong criticism. Although Nietzsche is considered to be an apostle of "will-to-power", yet by attainment of power or over-power, it is not possible to realize the human freedom. It is a natural thing which has to come of its own. Thus, as long as Nietzsche maintains that man is free, one can be in agreement with him. It is an agreed fact that human freedom has limits. It is limited by man's mental, physical and also due to the social environment in which he lives. Since man is a social being he has to realize his freedom living in this very society. He has to strictly adhere to the social norms and ideals of society and living there he can overcome all hindrances and then toll for his personal development through self-realization.

Summarizing, it can be said that in Nietzsche's philosophy though we do not find a straight forward discussion on human freedom, but it is quite discernable form his philosophical discussion that as a spiritual being is self-determined and free. He vehemently dismisses both free-will and determinism, to be a mere confusion in the study of human life. Nietzsche opines that man is not absolutely free. His freedom is limited by the physical mental and social environment but all along his life, man strives to do away with these limits and work for self-development, self-mastery through self-realization. For Nietzsche, God poses a hindrance in man's self-development and to be specific, in the realization of his freedom.

---

*Nietzsche is an atheist. He does not believe in the existence of God. He opines that God exhibits a hindrance to the man in realizing freedom. According to him, "unless God is dead, human freedom is incomplete". (Existentialism as philosophy, Fernado Molina, Prentice-hall Inc. 1962, P.28)

CHAPTER XXXIII

HUMAN RESPONSIBILITY

Nietzsche, who is an atheist, holds God to be the root cause of human problems. For Nietzsche, the death of God makes man alone responsible for the values with which he endows the earth. He says 'we deny God; we deny the responsibility in God'. He opines that man has the will to assume responsibility for himself.

It is a fundamental assumption of ethics that men are morally responsible for their actions. If this were not true, moral judgments would have no justification, we do not judge the motions of plants or inanimate objects to be moral or immoral, because they are rigidly determined by physical causes. We do not judge the actions of children and insane persons also to be moral or immoral, because their actions are not free. We hold adult human beings morally responsible for their actions. Thus, moral responsibility presupposes freedom of the will.

Responsibility etymologically means accountability or liability to be called upon to answer for an act done by a person. It implies that if he cannot reasonably defend his actions, he may justly be punished. A person freely performs an action, and is, therefore, responsible for it. Responsibility presupposes freedom. Determinism undermines responsibility.

If men were entirely determined by heredity and the environment without any power of initiative, they could not be held responsible for their actions; they could not be praised for their right actions or blamed for their wrong actions. Their actions would be on the same footing as physical events. But men are free to choose their ends and actions according to their idea of the highest good, and therefore responsible for their actions, though they are partly influenced by heredity and circumstances. If men are regarded as devoid of freedom, their actions cease to be moral or immoral. If they are creatures of circumstances, merit and demerit, right or wrong, virtues and vice, responsibility and punishability lose all their significance, morality becomes a myth.

Men are free; they are conscious of an ideal and freely realize it. They determine their own actions. They are not helpless creatures of circumstances. They are partly determined by circumstances but they freely respond to them accordingly to their characters. Circumstances are moulded by character; two persons living in the same environment have not the same circumstances. They take cognizance of those circumstances in the environment which fit in with their character and respond to them. Other circumstances do not influence their volition and actions. Men are responsible for their free voluntary actions. Responsibility implies freedom of the will.10

Freedom of the will means self-determinism. It does not mean indeterminism or liberty of indifference. Indeterminism holds that the self has the mysterious power of arbitrarily choosing between alternative possibilities or motives without any reason; the self has the power of undetermined choice. Indeterminism implies a power of absolutely undetermined choice in the self- a power of originating acts which have absolutely no connection with or relation to the self as it was before the act. Indeterminism undermines responsibility. If a free act is an absolutely new beginning undetermined by the character of the self, over which it has no control, the act is without any root in the self, and, consequently, the person cannot be held responsible for it. A person is not accountable for an act which he does not perform consciously and deliberately with a view to realizing his own chosen and through a chosen means. He is not responsible for the so-called free actions which spring from a mysterious power of arbitrary and undetermined choice within him over which he has no control.

Thus, determinism and indeterminism both undermines responsibility. Self-determinism is compatible with responsibility. Freedom of the will in the sense of self determinism can account for responsibility or accountability, physical compulsion, lack of reflection, subconscious compulsion under complexes, mental derangement or insanity are incompatible with responsibility.

Summarizing, it can be said that Nietzsche, being an atheist, holds God to be the primary cause of problems. Nietzsche denies the existence of God and also responsibility in him. He opines that death of God alone can make man responsible to the values with which he endows the earth. Nietzsche discusses the human responsibility from ethical view points and holds man morally responsible for their actions. He says responsibility implies freedom of the will. Freedom of the will is nothing but self-determinism. Nietzsche is not in agreement with determinists and indeterminists. Since both of them undermine responsibility. Only self-determinism is compatible with responsibility since it can only account for responsibility or accountability. Thus, concluding we can say that man has the will to assume responsibility for himself.

CHAPTER XXXIV

THE WILL-TO-POWER

Here an attempt will be made to explain Nietzsche's concept of will-to-power.

Nietzsche is an apostle of the will to power. The phrase 'will-to-power' appears late in Nietzsche's writings and then not at first as the most celebrated principle of his philosophy. Nietzsche's will to power must be considered central to his moral philosophy. In his book "ZARATHUSTRA" where the will to power is first pronounced as the basis of all morality, it is already that the greatest expression of power is to overcome oneself and it is the standard of self-overcoming which lies implicit in every morality.

The notion of "power", however, made its appearance long before Zarathustra, but Nietzsche first considered a will to power only in order to repudiate it. In "THE BIRTH OF TRAGEDY", Nietzsche notes that 'power is always evil', and it was the corruption of 'success and power' that became a theme for his work i.e., "HUMAN-ALL-TOO-HUMAN". Here, Nietzsche equates power with worldly power, and he is completely in agreement with his later philosophy. He takes all such power over others to be essentially demeaning the very contrary of what Zarathustra's will to power means to signify. Nietzsche's concept of will to power is specifically the potential to overcome.

Power is thus ability to overcome; the will to power is the drive to be strong, to be capable of overcoming. Power can refer to physical power to overcome physical obstacles, political power to overcome social obstacles, health to overcome diseases and mental power to solve problems. In short, power is the ability to overcome.

What is to be overcome? It is clear that Nietzsche's concept of power is more specific than this. All of these are manifestation of the will to power, but all powers are not equal. Physical power and good health are, for Nietzsche the lowest manifestation of will to power.

Nietzsche opines that pity, gratitude, humility and charity are taken to be expression for weakness of power rather than pure 'altruistic' or 'good motives' as generally understood. Nietzsche's views are criticized here. Although every morality is basically morality of power yet Nietzsche while distinguishing slave morality with master morality, made it a point that

Christianity which represents the slave morality carries with the qualities such as pity, gratitude, humility etc., which he considers to be the lowest manifestation of power. It can be pointed out here that Nietzsche's evaluation of these characteristics of Christianity is not at all proper. In fact, it is not the expression of weakness; it exhibits the inner strength or power of a man to cultivate such qualities or characteristics. It is discernable that experiencing such things needs an inner power which is nothing but the highest degree of perfection, pleasure and happiness and in turn he will cultivate the good nature within himself and also the good motives. Thus, we can say that every human being in his actions and values, along with Christianity is striving for more and more power in order to transform themselves into master morality. Nietzsche further committed a mistake in dividing the will to power improperly i.e., 'lowest' and 'highest' form of will to power. He seems to be wrong in placing the physical power and good health in the 'lower' category of will to power. Since having power in itself carries a positive meaning and having good inner will only keep the man to maintain his physical power or stamina and in turn good health. Had he put the poor health or poor physical strength in the lower category of will to power then to certain extent one could be in agreement with Nietzsche but not otherwise? Thus, it can be said emphatically that Nietzsche is wrong in not calling the good health and physical strength, the higher if not the highest will to power.

The highest will to power (sometimes called "true power") is self-overcoming. From above discussion of his concern for morality, we are already prepared to understand this in attaining mastery through sublimation, of the passion by reason. Nietzsche's self-overcoming and will to power are ultimately the Socratic pursuit of rationality. Nietzsche insisting the importance of rationality, control by reason that he takes philosophy, the 'will- to truth' to be 'the most spiritual will to power' and takes strength to be a good only in so far as reason involved.

Heidegger on the other hand, relating power to freedom says that power and freedom are ontological dimensions. The ontological analysis of the human reality demands not only a consideration of freedom but also of power. Power is manifested in the state while freedom is the realization of the uniqueness of man. Man is involved in and introduced to both freedom and power. He is inseparable from the state in so far as he is a political being but separable in the creativity of his individuality.

Man is aware of power in the state, he is conscious of its distortive and destructive possibility. Not only does man realize the distortive and distinctive possibility of power in the state, but he is involved I the same distortive and destructive possibility within himself.

Heidegger thus discusses power only in political terms that is the power of state, its distortive and destructive nature which is practiced by man himself.

Karl Jaspers' views on power are also political in nature. Jaspers opines that power is the tension between societies and state he says, man living in society, cannot apprehend in freedom to act and to realize it. There is an unceasing tension between mass order for the supply of necessities and the decision is based on power which arises in collaboration. Everything is left to be decided by the divine authority of state. And it develops a sort of tension between the society and the state.

Karl Jaspers, too, thus discusses power only in political terms of society and state., the relation between the two and the tension arising thereafter out of the collaboration between the two i.e., society and state, of course for the fulfillment of the needs and demands of man and society in large.

Heidegger and Jaspers agree that Nietzsche's doctrine of the will to power is a radical experiment in communication. Furthermore, Heidegger reminds us, as does Jaspers, for as Nietzsche himself says "will is merely a word". Like Jaspers, Heidegger notes that Nietzsche, sometimes speaks of the will to power as life and that at other times, he speaks of life as one form of the will to power; but also, like Jaspers, Heidegger fails to distinguish between the metaphysical doctrine of the will to power and the doctrine of the will to power as philosophical anthropology. For Heidegger, Nietzsche's philosophy is metaphysics with occasional excursions into the mundane world, whereas for Jaspers, Nietzsche's philosophy is philosophical anthropology with occasional excursions into metaphysics. To me Nietzsche's doctrine of the will to power is nothing but a philosophy of improving man's inner capability living in this very mundane world.

Man is yet a central fact of this universe. Living in this world, man has to work upon in order to improve his quality of life. Man can make best use of the will to power to mend his life according to requirements. It is not enough to live long but live well is the utmost need of the hour. Will to power can certainly bring certain changes in the lives of men, if worked upon properly. Will to power is synonym of life and vice-versa. Since life can be lived only in this very world therefore life has no import apart from this world. This man and the world are complementary to each other and also closely related to each other.

Summarizing, it can be said that Nietzsche's doctrine of will to power makes him really an apostle. According to him will power is nothing but ability to overcome i.e., overcoming of the physical, mental, social and even political obstacles. To be more specific man's self-overcoming is only will to power.

Nietzsche's views on power underwent a radical change from "THE BIRTH OF TRAGEDY" where he took power to be only an evil, to the "ZARATHUSTRA" where he reached to a conclusion that self-overcoming of hindrances or obstacles is will to power. Will to power is also an expression of morality which helps man to improve upon the quality of life while living in the universe. He can certainly bring changes and improvement thereafter. Will to power creates in a man a sense of striving for more and more power and in turn helping him to attain the highest degree of perfection, pleasure and happiness. Man becomes altruistic and also carries good motives with himself.

Nietzsche's will to power is thus far removed from the common imagery of military strength. He says 'the most powerful are not the politicians and soldiers, but the artists, the philosophers and the aesthete, will to power is ultimately control over oneself; it is not license but restraint; not power to hurt or destroy but power to create.

Heidegger and Karl Jaspers have discussed the 'power' only in terms of political power. According to Heidegger the sphere of power belongs to state, carrying with it the distortions and destructive nature, of course practiced by man himself.

Karl Jaspers on the other hand opines that power creates a tension between the society and the state. Tension aroused due to collaborate between the two in the process of fulfilling the needs and demands of man and society in large. Thus, it can be seen that in the field of 'will to power' Nietzsche is left alone, since Heidegger and Nietzsche have been, too political, while discussing the power.

CHAPTER XXXV

NIETZSCHE'S CONCEPT OF SUPERMAN

Nietzsche's vision of the superman is one of the most fascinating aspects of his philosophy, as well as the most misinterpreted. With the doctrine of superman, we get the other half of Nietzsche's theory of man; man understood as possibility. Nietzsche's concept of will to power culminated into his concept of superman. It is only through will to power that he decided to overcome and in overcoming he overcomes the whole of mankind and becomes the superman.

Nietzsche opines that the world will not be right and man will not come to his own till the sense of lordship and power, the instinct of mastery and strength are not sensed by an in particulars and mankind in general, he ousted such feelings as pity, generosity, sympathy and sacrifice. The real test of man in a group is energy, capacity and power. The world should be made to exit for the strong, the great and the few. The goal of human efforts should be development of finer and stronger individuals and not the elevation of all. The superman not mankind is the goal. It is the height of stupidity to think of mankind or to undertake its improvement. Mankind does not exist; it is an abstraction. Here it is discernable from the statement of Nietzsche that he seems to have forgotten the very principles of democracy. Democracy takes pride in providing an equal opportunity to all. Men living under it develop their overall personality and flourish in all fields. Though democracy is not practiced all over the world but since time immemorial peoples have strived to make democracy their way of life. A few achieved this objective and others are on its way in realizing democracy. Democracy is a system of running government. The United States of America is the form of Govt. by the people, for the people and of the people. That means democracy in all respect takes care of its people. Thus, for Nietzsche, our conscious endeavour should be to bring into existence a new type of men; the race of supermen. Its mission should be to rule, and not to serve.

From the very beginning we must keep in mind that the superman is not to be conceived of as a state which man can achieve. One never is a superman except in a relative sense. *

According to Nietzsche the first step on the path to superman is the overcoming of radical nihilism. This opens up the possibility for the creation of new values. It becomes clear in terms of the doctrine of the superman hat even though there is a general framework and hierarchy of values; particular values are to be determined dialectically with reference to the struggle of self-overcoming.

At first, "Nietzsche spoke as if his hope were for the production of a new species. Later he came to think of his superman as the superior individual rising precariously out of the mire of mass mediocrity, and owing his existence more to selective breeding and careful nurture than to the hazards of natural selection. The superman can survive only by human selection in order to produce fine offspring also by providing them with noble education.

Without good birth, nobility is impossible. Given good birth and eugenic is a severe schooling where perfection will be exacted, as a matter of course, not even meriting praises; where there will be few comforts and many responsibilities, where the body will be taught to suffer in silence, and the will may learn to obey and to command since obedience only gives the right to command. A man so born and bred would be beyond good and evil. Such man would be brave, fearless and his goodness will always increase the feeling of power, the will to power in man. Nietzsche opines, perhaps the dominant mark of the superman will be love of danger and strife, provided they have a purpose. He will not seek safety first; he will leave happiness to the greatest number.

Energy, intellect, pride and power constitute the superman but they must be harmonized, the passions will become power only when they are selected the unified by some great purpose which moulds a chaos of desires into the power of personality.12

Zarathustra is the teacher of the doctrine of the superman, but at the same time he himself is on the path to the superman. Here again we must be careful, for there is no single path to the superman, each has his own path as a self-overcoming. This new vision of man depends upon two forms of freedom. The first is the freedom from nihilism, that is, the belief in transcendence and the second is the freedom to create, for it is only in creating as a willing and valuing that self-over-coming is possible.

The two great virtues of the superman are honesty and nobility. Nietzsche placed an extremely high value upon honesty. He says, "Take good care there, you higher man. For nothing today is more precious to me and rarer than honesty. Nietzsche's concept of honesty is inextricably bound up with strength. Self-overcoming is a willing that is simultaneously a commanding and an obeying, grounded in a strict, even severe, sense of honesty with oneself. This includes a merciless recognition of one's own weaknesses and limitations.

Needless to say, this honesty also applies to one's relation with others. Here there is something of a problem, for Nietzsche's description is not always consistent and he himself sometimes forgets that the superman is not a type. From these various descriptions get a picture of the superman as a man with incredible sensitivity and yet a kind of hardness and strength that verges on insensitivity. In part this is a result of Nietzsche's own extreme sensitivity coupled within his obsession concerning health and strength both physical and spiritual. Nietzsche was aware of the immense difficulty of bringing about such a fusion.

Here I must say, though, Nietzsche allocates the very best of qualities such as nobility and honesty too the superman but he disregards the whole of mankind. He is bent upon developing energy, intellect, pride and power in a few of chosen individuals, who in long run may not prove worth to the society. Nietzsche must develop a sense of understanding, and maturity in his thoughts and must aspire to develop all these virtues in the whole of mankind. If each individual is trained to cultivate good habits, nobility and honesty and also can improve upon the energy, intellect, pride and power thus making every individual a specimen of society. Individuals will learn the principles of mutual co-existence and they will also develop the intimate relations with each other. The society will automatically improve and thus the whole of mankind. We must make it a point that we always work for the improvement of society in order to have a better living.

Commenting on Nietzsche's concept of superman, Karl Jaspers, firstly, prepares the ground for discussion of the superman in a very interesting way. He argues that the notion of creation is absolutely fundamental in Nietzsche's philosophy. Jasper's exposition is especially valuable in that he points out all the various meaning and levels of meaning contained in Nietzsche's notion of creation. Jaspers says that the notion of creation remains necessarily indefinite. It is perfectly intelligible, but only within the context of the whole of Nietzsche's philosophy. Jaspers emphasizing the distinction between the superior man and the super man says that superior men have already appeared in history, but the superman has not yet arrived.

Nietzsche modified his conception of the 'political' and social roles which would 'permit' the superman to exist in his own context as the self-creating being in a relationship of mutual tolerance between the superman must achieve the power to transform the nature of social and 'political' instructions. Thus, the possibilities of superman come to depend upon a co-existence. Ultimately the doctrine of superman brings with it the vision of a new kind of humanity and the superman becomes the 'legislator' of the future. Nietzsche gradually comes to the conclusion that the superman must also create the conditions for his own self overcoming.

Summarizing, it can be said that Nietzsche's superman is not feasible in the present society. In fact, Nietzsche expects too much of superman. He makes superman a supreme authority forgetting the very mankind. Nietzsche's views seem politically motivated. Nietzsche's own aspiration to attain the highest in the political through his self-overcoming and will to power made him to think of superman. In fact, in his lifetime, he could not utter very clearly that he himself has chosen the path to be a superman and that he is a superman though he made every effort to be at par with Goethe and other great personality of his time but failed miserably in his attempt to be a superman.

In fact, he should have concentrated making mankind superb instead choosing a superman out of the very mankind and develop him thereafter.

In the modern context, mankind, not the superman is the need of the hour. Mankind should be given an opportunity to exist in harmony by developing good virtues like honesty and nobility and also improving upon the energy a, intellect, pride and power.

---

*Nietzsche's conception of the superman may be contrasted with Aurobindo conception of superman Aurobindo believes that new human society will be evolved by spiritually transformed men or supermen, who will completely surrender their will to the divine will, eschew love and hatred transcend egoism, rise above intellect and intellectual morality, identify themselves with mankind, and become conscious instruments of the will and energy of God. They will work with the supra mind, and bring down the kingdom of God on earth. This concept may seem to be utopian and unrealizable, but Aurobindo believes that it is inescapable and irresistible.

HUMAN LIBERTY AND RESPONSIBILITY IN MARTIN HEIDEGGER'S PHILOSOPHY

CHAPTER XXXVI

MARTIN HEIDEGGER (1899-1976): Brief Sketch and Introduction

MARTIN HEIDEGGER (1899-1976)

Martin Heidegger
Heidegger in 1960

Born
26 September 1889, Meßkirch, Baden, German Empire
Died
26 May 1976 (aged 86), Meßkirch, West Germany
Education
Collegium Borromaeum [de], (1909–1911)[1]
University of Freiburg, (PhD, 1914; Dr. phil. hab. 1916)
Spouse(s)
Elfride Petri (m. 1917)

Partner(s)

Elisabeth Blochmann (1918–1969), Hannah Arendt (1924–1928)

Era

20th-century philosophy

Region

Western philosophy

School

Continental philosophy, Phenomenology, Hermeneutics, Ontological hermeneutics[2]
Hermeneutic phenomenology (early)[3], Transcendental hermeneutic phenomenology (late)[4], Existentialism, Existential phenomenology[5]

Institutions

University of Marburg, University of Freiburg

Theses

- *Die Lehrevom Urteil imPsychologismus. Ein kritisch-theoretischerBeitragzur Logik (The Doctrine of Judgment in Psychologism: A Critical-theoretical Contribution to Logic)* (1914)
- *Die Kategorien- und Bedeutungslehre des Duns Scotus (Duns Scotus's Doctrine of Categories and Meaning)* (1916)

Doctoral advisor

Arthur Schneider (PhD advisor), Heinrich Rickert (Dr. phil. hab. advisor)

Doctoral students

Hans Jonas

Main interests

- Ontology, Christian philosophy, Metaphysics, Art, Greek philosophy, Technology
- Language, Poetry, Thinking

Notable ideas

- Heideggerian terminology, *Dasein*, *Gestell*, Ontotheology, Ontological difference
- Existentials (*Existenzialien*), *Ekstase*, Sigetics (*Sigetik*), Hermeneutic circle, *Aletheia*

- Disclosure, Fundamental ontology, Forgetfulness of Being (*Seinsvergessenheit*)
- Dwelling (*Wohnen*), Language as the vehicle through which the question of Being can be unfolded[6], "Language speaks", Art's ability to set up a strife between "world" and "earth"[7]

Influences

- Anaximander, Aquinas, Aristotle, Augustine, Brentano, Dilthey, Thomas of Erfurt[8], Hartmann, Hegel
- Heraclitus, Hölderlin, Husserl, Jaspers, Kant, Kierkegaard, Laozi[9], Lask[10], Nietzsche, Parmenides
- Plato, Rickert, Duns Scotus, Jakob von Uexküll[11], Count Yorck

Influenced

- Agamben, Arendt, Beaufret, de Beauvoir, Blanchot, Borgmann, Bultmann, Derrida, Dreyfus, Dugin
- El-Bizri, Foucault, Gadamer, Habermas, Harman, Jaspers, Jonas, Kuki, Levinas, Löwith, Marcel, Marcuse, Marion, Meillassoux, Merleau-Ponty, Nancy, Norberg-Schulz, Patočka, Rahner, Rorty
- Sartre, Schürmann, Sloterdijk, Stiegler, Strauss, Zubiri

Courtesy -- Wikipedia

MARTIN HEIDEGGER

Martin Heidegger was born in 1889. He belongs to the Black Forest region and comes from a catholic peasant family. He was actively interested from early youth in western theology and philosophy. In 1915, he got a lectureship in philosophy at Friedberg, where he came under the influence of Husserl, who was professor of philosophy there from 1916-29. Heidegger made a reputation as a stimulating and original teacher and was appointed to the chair of philosophy at Marburg in 1923, where he wrote "SEIN AND ZEIT", published in 1927. He returned to Friedberg to succeed Husserl in 1929. He was elected Rector in 1933 after Hitler came to power, and resigned the post early in the following year. Heidegger living in the rude solitude of a skiing hut, up in the mountain of the Black Forest, died in 1976.

INTRODUCTION

Martin Heidegger insistently dissociates himself from existential philosophy, for he is concerned with the problem of being, not with personal existence and its ethical interests, the human condition as such. For all that, he is inescapably put amongst the existentialists because he is one of them in his themes and ideas and in his treatment of the problems and in the language, he uses, as well in his debt to Kierkegaard and the influence he exercised upon others, especially Sartre.

Like Kierkegaard, Heidegger too, was brought up religiously, although he remained virtually an atheist throughout his life. The Kierkegaardian influence continues to be pronounced throughout his philosophy. Heidegger, like Kierkegaard, argues that conceptual analysis is not sufficient to give us knowledge of what actually exists and what does not.

In spite of an obvious difference in style between Kierkegaard and Heidegger, we find a great many of Kierkegaard's central ideas expanded in the heavy academic formulations of "Sein and Zeit" (Being and time). Both have the concern with individual human existence. This leads both of them into an attack on conceptual analysis particular analysis of 'human nature'. They both maintain that the "real self" is "ethical, not cognitive".

Here attention will be focused on Heidegger's first great "Existentialist" work, "Being and Time". He himself claims that the project of "Being and Time" remains his central concern.

CHAPTER XXXVII

QUINTESSENCE OF EXISTENCE

Heidegger is the philosopher of the "Dasein" (a term used for 'being') which is nothing but existence. Heidegger like Kierkegaard insists that freedom of choice and recognition of this freedom is the very essence of existence.

Before discussing Heidegger's views on human existence in detail, first Kierkegaard's views on human existence in detail, first Kierkegaard's views on human existence, will be briefly stated in order to show Heidegger's indebtedness to Kierkegaard, the father of existentialism.

As mentioned earlier (chapter two), Kierkegaard is concerned only with a particular kind of existence, namely, individual human existence, Kierkegaard speaks of individual existence in a very special sense, a sense in which a man is not simply a biological, psychological, or social animal. But in which a man is a 'human being', an existence which is something far more exciting than the "mere existence' of a particular organism. This notion of "existence" is reserved for those who live as individuals, not biologically but individually in their thought and their values.

Kierkegaard affirms that man does not 'prove' his own existence to himself but only 'encounters' it. Man is involved in his existence. The very core of human existence is its concreteness and subjectivity which can be grasped by man only from the very act of 'existing'.

Man's encounter with his existence takes place when he has to choose decisively for a life time between the alternatives of authentic and unauthentic existence. Man has to choose between these alternatives with his whole being, and the choice he makes, he chooses himself or the kind of existence he is going to live. Man, thus confronts his existence in the exercise of his freedom to choose. Man's whole being is involved in his choice and the choice he makes, decides the level of existence. Either he chooses ethico-religious existence, enters upon an inward commitment to God and thereby he realizes that he is an 'existing' individual, or he completely loses himself in objective pleasures and thereby forgets that he is an 'existing' individual. In this existential choice man does not chose anything outside himself but chooses himself either to exist as a unique individual or not to exist so.

Heidegger's interest in 'existence/ is essentially different from that of either Kierkegaard or Jaspers. He regarded it as his task to analyze. Being (Human existence) ontologically in this respect 'Existence' seemed to him the fundamental characteristics of being. Heidegger is concerned with the "existentialistic structure" of the being with what is basic to 'existence'. His aim is to analyze the structure of human existence as it actually is, in its relation to the things in the "world", non-human and human.

Heidegger as a philosopher of being is primarily concerned with man's being in the world not only as a mind but as concrete being. Being in the world; reveals human reality. The being as the kind of "Dasein" is in its being as towards its own possibility. It chooses and decides and it may gain or may lose itself, in as far as its being is concerned. Two fundamental modes of being, authentically and in authenticity are distinguished, both of them depending on the fact that "being" is essentially always my own.

The characteristic of being are not qualities but possible ways of "being". Therefore, the term "Dasein" (being) is too express not its "essence", but the "being", it means "being there". To distinguish further the kind of being, the term 'existence' is applied exclusively to it.

"Being" which is here taken to mean the same as life, and "existence", which is of an absolute significance to the individual? Human being is characterized is "being-in-the-world". Heidegger wants to differentiate the sense in which being is, from the sense in which, things, events, states, properties are said to be. The sense of "to be" in which being is, therefore will be called "existence" possessing and understanding of being including an understanding of human being. *

Thus, we see that Heidegger emphasized that man exists in the form of 'being' in the world. "To be" in the world is ultimately called man's existence in the world. Existence of man only shows its presence in the world. Existing in this very world, man makes choices and thus his freedom of choices makes him to choose either authentic or inauthentic mode of human existence. In both the authentic and inauthentic modes man relates himself to the world. The only difference between them is that while in the authentic existence man deals with the world having in view the whole structure of his existence including in itself its future possibilities, Man ignores them in his inauthentic existence and 'loses' himself in the present preoccupation of every day existence.

Heidegger being atheistic existentialist is not in agreement with Kierkegaard's ethico-religious and the aesthetic levels of human existence.

Heidegger remains silent on man's inward commitment to God, and the freedom and responsibility thereof.

Heidegger has disassociated himself from other existentialists who believed in the presence of human nature. According to Heidegger, there is no 'human nature' and there are, therefore no given human endeavors. Heidegger further maintains that we do not derive our meaning from the world (there is human nature), but rather than the world derives its meaning from us. It is interesting to note that Heidegger following Husserl, in explaining non-existence of human nature, who maintains that we 'constitute the significance of the world"; though Heidegger has accepted that this recognition is a shaking of the foundations of our very lives.

---

*On Being Human, Richard Schmitt. P.15

CHAPTER XXXVIII

HUMAN POSSIBILITIES

Heidegger's views on human possibilities may be discussed here. Since existence is the projection of possibilities, so we must enquire into the nature of these possibilities and the nature of this projection. It is important to note that Heidegger maintains that "Existence is possibility". He does not say that existence has possibilities. Existence is the possibility and necessity of choosing oneself, of formulating a concept of oneself. It can be said, a possibility is a choice, and it is an alternative which can be chosen by human being. A possibility need not present us with a choice as such as we can see from some of Heidegger's examples. He speaks, for example, of 'possible' and 'impossible, possibilities as well as necessary possibility. If possibility is necessary; then it is not possible to have a choice as to whether we shall adopt it or not; death is such a necessary possibility. *

A human being is his own possibility. This means that we should not expect to find a general set of potentialities or capacities for all human beings. According to Heidegger, there is no 'human nature', and there are, therefore, no given human endeavors. Heidegger adds that there is not a priori Justification for man; choosing one end over another and not a priori reason for expecting that men will tend to choose one end over another.

A possibility for Heidegger is any structure of the world e.g., a horizon, a set of "limiting images". For Heidegger, possibilities are not just possibilities for experience or possibilities for knowing. There are also possibilities for actions, possibilities for moods, attitudes, and feelings. Possibilities are possible structures of being in the world, and these are possible simply by virtue of the fact that they can be conceived by human being. Possibility, for Heidegger, is contemplable structure for being in the world. Because of the peculiar structure of human being in the world, any structure of being-in the-world is a structure of beings itself.

In spite of the indefinitely large number of possibilities available to human beings (which are his existence, these possibilities are based on a simple pair of possibilities, the possibility of being authentic (winning oneself and the possibility of being in-authentic (losing oneself). These possibilities are of a very different nature, the various "possibilities" or goals such as being an artist, musician or apolitical figure etc., on which men may disagree.

These possibilities are essential to human beings' existence; they are the very nature of existence. Authenticity and in-authenticity are possibilities concerning the manner of human beings choosing among possibilities in general. The explicit and honest recognition of the necessity of making choice is authenticity; the refusal to recognize one's choice (as one's own) is in-authenticity. Existence is possibility and therefore the one 'possibility' which is not open to human being is to give up his possibilities.

Human beings always understand themselves; to their existence, in terms of a possibility of themselves; to be themselves or not to be themselves. Human beings have either chosen these possibilities themselves, or got themselves into them, or grown up in them already. Human being decides his existence. Human beings cannot be said to have only logical and physical possibilities. Human possibilities are more intimately connected with them than logical and physical possibilities. Human beings determine, in certain ways, their nature possibilities and that is why Heidegger keeps insisting that being human is "being able to be".[1]

Thus, we see that Heidegger clearly states his views on human possibilities of authenticity, in-authenticity and various other possibilities described above. He discriminates between possibility and possibilities. He further makes a distinction between authentic and inauthentic modes of existence and the possibilities thereof; possibilities refer to human beings' relationship to himself and also to their existence in the world. Living in this very world, human beings determine their possibilities; Human beings make choices and in making choices they chose the best possibility for them. Human beings continuously strive to lead a life which gives them a sense of satisfaction from within.

---

*Death is human beings' ultimate possibility. Though death is a necessary possibility, yet we cannot choose our own death. Therefore, it can be said that 'possibility' does not simply mean 'something which can be chosen or not chosen by human beings. Similarly, there are 'impossible possibilities' for example, the impossibility of immortality, or the impossibility in our wish to be God. Yet it is one of our possibilities in the requisite sense. (From Rationalism to Existentialism, Solomon Robert C, P. 212)

CHAPTER XXXIX

AUTHENTIC AND INAUTHENTIC EXISTENCE

Heidegger views on Human existence will be discussed here. Heidegger tells us that there are two modes of existence of human beings. These are:

i. Authenticity &
ii. In-authenticity.

Authenticity and in-authenticity refer to "a man's relationship to himself". The authentic man thinks and acts in terms of an adequate understanding of himself whereas the inauthentic man acts blindly. Both authenticity and in-authenticity are every human being's possibility; it is not the case that some men are 'naturally' authentic and others are not, authenticity depend on an adequate ontological recognition of one's existence, facticity and fallenness (Bondage). In-authenticity neglects existence and lives in fallenness (Bondage). It is clear that authenticity is something to be striven for. *

Heidegger explains how human beings attain authentic mode of human existence from in-authentic mode of human existence using the freedom. The Heidegger's distinction between the authentic and the inauthentic mode of human existence can well be understood in terms of the mode of concealment.

The inauthentic mode of existence is not so much a description of what man is but of what he has chosen to be. Human being, as they chose to be inauthentic being, they remain in this state for a stipulated time and then make free choices and become authentic being.

Human beings make use of "freedom" to convert themselves from inauthentic mode of existence to authentic mode of human existence. This freedom remains concealed during the inauthentic mode of existence and this is always retained by human beings. Under no circumstances this freedom should be lost. It will not be out of place to discuss the characteristics of the authentic mode of human existence and the inauthentic mode of human existence. First, we will see how Heidegger characterizes authentic existence and then it can be related to the inauthentic existence.

Heidegger characterizes authentic existence by three "modes or behavior" of human beings towards the world. (1) Discovery of oneself as already in the world, which is the recognition of one's existence. (2) Understanding, which is the projection of possibilities regarding one's attitude and projects towards the world? (3) Discourse, which is the capacity to articulate.

These three characteristics of authenticity have their counterparts in the characterization of in-authenticity.[2]

The inauthentic man does not 'discover himself in the world; but rather finds himself in a state of ambiguity, caught up in the whirlpool of daily 'endless' (meaningless) activity.

Heidegger described the average everydayness of human existence as its state of (bondage), from its own authentic potentiality-of-being; in the state of (bondage) man's potentiality of being enters the modes of in-authenticity. In his state of bondage, man does not think for himself and does not fully conceive of any personal goal or possibility which he has to specially realize for himself by the exercise of his own potentialities, but blindly accepts what is said by others and is guided by public opinion in his decision and actions. Constant craving for public approval results in his blind conformity to public opinion, and this is the characteristic of man's inauthentic modes of human existence which marks his 'losses of personal freedom.

Man's loss of freedom is supported by a false sense of tranquility and security in his state of bondage which he misinterprets as a case of progress or ascending. The state of bondage is characterized by 'idle talk', 'curiosity' and 'ambiguity' and freedom from these is essential if man has to re-orient himself towards the realization of his own potentiality-of-being.

Dread manifests itself in man's flight from personal responsibility and discloses to him his 'bondage' from authentic existence in the world. Conscious awakens man to the necessity of facing and accepting dread by orienting his existence towards the authentic realization of his potentiality of being. The kind of being which man has oriented toward the realization of his potentiality-of-being is being-oneself as distinguished from the state of bondage in which he considers himself to be one like-many. The kind of being oriented towards the realization of potentiality-of-being is the authentic mode of existence described as 'being-free' as distinguished from being-lost, which is characteristic of the inauthentic mode of existence.

Heidegger thus described 'freedom' as the characteristic of the authentic mode of human existence. Man becomes 'free' to the extent that he distinguishes himself from the inauthentic mode of human existence characterized by his bondage and lostness. Man analyses an authentic mode of human existence by orienting his life towards realization of his potentiality-of-being. Thus, in short, it can be said that authentic life is the recognition of the responsibility and the opened range of choice. That means one always has a concern of his own 'mode of existence'. Whereas, inauthentic life is the refusal to recognize the responsibility and one's choices.

---

*Heidegger warns us that authenticity can only be an ideal for us. Every man is structured by the tendency towards bondage, and every action will be tinged with in-authenticity. Although authenticity is the goal, Heidegger stresses the most people strive against it; their fundamental tendency is to refuse to recognize themselves. (BEING AND TIME, MARTIN HEIDEGGER, P. 143)

CHAPTER XL

HUMAN LIBERTY AND RESPONSIBILITY

Heidegger himself has stated that his position in philosophy is radically different from that of his contemporaries JP Sartre and Karl Jaspers.

Heidegger's concept of freedom comes to light in his distinction between the authentic and inauthentic modes of human existence. Man's freedom consists in his exercise of personal choice so as to cultivate, develop and realize his own inherent potentiality-of-being, and this freedom is 'lost' when he subordinates all his decisions and actions to the approval of public opinion.

Freedom, for Heidegger, is the characteristic of the authentic mode of human existence, which belongs to man. Man becomes 'free' to the extent that he distinguishes himself from the inauthentic mode of human existence. In both the authentic and the inauthentic modes man relates himself to the world in terms of concernful dealings with it. The only difference between them is that while in the authentic modes of existence men concernfully deals with the world having in view the whole structure of his existence including in-itself and its future possibilities. He ignores them in his inauthentic existence and 'loses' himself in the present pre-occupations of everyday existence. Man's activity in authentic existence is always, guided by them. Since his own 'existence' which he ignores does not count; but in authentic existence it is guided by what he has to say to himself in view of realizing the future responsibilities of his own existence.

Heidegger employs the concepts of conscious, guilt and analysis, in describing the concept of freedom. Conscience is the silent call of 'care' which awakens man to analyze the choice in order to live the life of authentic existence of freedom in the face of possibility of death; it also discloses man's guilt, which consists in his responsibility for his being-in-the world, and as pertaining to his being-in –the world. It is the ground of both his good and bad actions. Man does not become guilty by his action but is guilty as committed to and responsible for his being-in-the world, and it is because of his existential 'guilt' or basic commitment to being-in-the-world that he is capable of moral guilt or goodness. The existential guilt in the sense of being committed to and responsible for his finite and contingent being-in-the world must be accepted by man if he is to recognize his existence in the world and live an authentic life without avoiding his personal responsibility.

The life of freedom which the individual resolves to live is not a superior state of being and does not promise an entity into any supra-human level of existence. Freedom is not a metaphysical but a mundane concept, and the life of freedom is to be lived by the individual on the earth. As a lived reality, it is related to all the three aspects of human existence, namely, it being-ahead-of itself (future), being thrown (past) and being fallen (present). The life of freedom is human existence oriented towards the future realization of its highest potentiality-of-being, and it necessarily implies the individual's acceptance of responsibility for his past 'throw-ness'. Acceptance of the past and orientation towards the 'future' subordinates the 'present' everydayness to a complete change in the light of the individual's being free for the realization of his possibilities.

Heidegger's analysis of the concept of death further clarifies his conception of freedom as based on that distinction between authentic and inauthentic modes of human existence. *

Freedom pertains to man's authentic acceptance of death because of his being-in-the-world whereby he takes personal charge of hi being-in-the-world as being ahead of itself towards death and refuses to be deceived by the illusions of permanence and security of his everyday existence.

On the other hand, his contemporary, Karl Jasper's self is freedom in its subjectivity and solitude which consciously distinguishes itself from all its objective expressions and is oriented towards transcendence. Jasper's notion of the being-oneself closely resembles, another contemporary of Heidegger, JP Sartre's notion of the "POUR-SOI" (Being-for-itself). Neither of them identifies the self with the externalized reflective consciousness but both conceive of it as the basic freedom which exists always as a possibility by consciously distinguishing itself from its own actual identification with the world. Both Jaspers and Sartre extended the notions of man's freedom beyond his subject-object pattern of existence. Both emphasized the need for awakening man to his own 'authentic-existence', to the awareness of his own freedom and personal responsibility, and both regarded the admission of religious authority as an attack on one's personal freedom. But there is a fundamental difference between them. Sartre's "POUR-SOI" (Being-for-itself) is helplessly pitched against the "EN-SOI" (Being-in-itself) in which it endlessly struggles to realize itself but is incapable of doing so securely because of its own tendency towards separation and the corresponding transiency of its own realization in the "EN-SOI" (Being-in-itself".

Karl Jaspers maintains that man gets frustrated in the world because of the 'limitations' in the world. Whereas Sartre regards that the universe is not basically meaningless, purposeless and absurd. It is an indirect-manifestation of transcendence and absurd. It is an indirect-manifestation of transcendence and thus serves as the field for man's self-exercise as freedom tending; towards an encounter with transcendence.

Human existence is essentially constituted by human activity. Heidegger combines 'freedom' with 'activity' by emphasizing renunciation in action instead of renunciation of action, and this ethical description of freedom is desirable from Heidegger's ontological description of freedom as constitute of human existence.

Thus, like Sartre, Heidegger also believes that freedom, in the sense of the inherent 'nothingness' of human existence is basically the ontological 'truth' of human existence and that the practice of this 'truth' in man's authentic existence manifests itself as his ethical or moral life. For both, Heidegger and Sartre, to be 'true' to one's existence is also to be ethical and moral.

With regard to Heidegger's concern towards responsibility, it can be seen that there is an inauthentic counterpart to all the authentic ways of experiencing concern towards the world. It is possible that a man can go through the whole of his life in the inauthentic state, and he may never emerge from it. But reflection may bring his attention to the true state of affairs and may open his eyes to his position in the world. This position is above all a position of responsibility.

Man realizes his unique position in the world as a human being. Man comes to realize further that it is he and he alone who are responsible for the world. Man's connection with the world is necessarily that of concern (since man has ambitions, regards some things as hindrances, some as aids to himself). Man, further accepts the significance which everyone else attaches to things. When man sees the truth about himself, he sees that people in general cannot really be the source of significance for his life. Thus, man finds himself alone in the world. Slowly man determinedly changes the character of his concern for the world, and keeping before his eyes his lonely and responsible position; he exercised resolution and launches himself forward into authentic existence.

Summarizing, it can be said that for Heidegger, freedom is the characteristic of authentic existence. Freedom is nothing but personal choice of a man which helps man to cultivate, develop and realize his own inherent potentiality–of-being. And this very realization makes man to feel responsible for his acts. Man existing in this world should live an authentic mode of life without feeling from his personal responsibility and this only a true living of a man and the very purpose of human existence.

---

*The existentialist concepts and the Hindu philosophical system, G. Srinivasan, P. 165

CHAPTER XLI

INTER RELATIONS OF PEOPLE

Heidegger's main concern in "SEIN ND ZEIT" (Existence and being) is the problem of 'being' in general. It is far from clear, what this problem is, but at any rate the approach to its solution is said to be through the consideration of the nature of man, who stands in a particular relation to being as a whole, because of his unique ability to raise question about it. Man is the only being in the world that is capable of considering the nature of being as on whole and is therefore in a unique way exposed to it. Man is defined as 'potential existence'. This is to say that man is always transcending what he is at any given moment. He is always stretching towards the future and aiming at something which he is not yet. Furthermore, "man is not a being in isolation". His existence is "existence-in-the-world", and so he is conditioned, in every mode of his thought and action, not only by the material situation in which he finds himself but also, crucially, by other people in the world. Being bound up with the other people is an essential mode of the existence of each of us. The being of man is 'being with'; Men live together in this very world and consider themselves as members of a society group. This very group is mankind at large. Heidegger draws a distinction between authentic and inauthentic existence of men living in the form of a social group. To accept one's role as a kind of generalized man, as totally part of the social group, to be content with this, is to live in-authentically. It is possible, on the other hand, to seek, to realize one's possibilities as an individual alone; and as if one were isolated and independent. This is authentic existence.[3]

Heidegger maintains that man is primarily a social being, a being-with-others. The problem of existentialism is not man's loneliness, but the restrictive inauthentic ties he forms with others. The thrust of Heidegger's existentialism is to force us to break some of those ties with others. Man is first the good citizen, the average human being, the everyday being. The task of existential questioning is to let him loose from this social framework and allow him to find his own possibilities, or his authentic self. Man is primarily concerned about himself, his own 'self'. In order to know other selves, one must first learn to appreciate one-self. My being-in-the-world, of being constituted by my projects and by my relations with the objects involve my being-with-others who are also in the world, of being the existence of others is a necessity and is constitutive of my being and implied in it. For example, as the teacher; the teacher implies the student; and as the needle; needle implies both eth thread and the cloth; the nature of being is being-in-common, human existence is a shared existence in primordial and constitutive of full self-consciousness and self-affirmation derived from my consciousness of others.

Our initial experience of others is not an experience of things; but neither do we first encounter the other as a person rather, our first encounter with another is much like our primary encounter with the world as equipment. Others are to be employed to serve purposes; however, ne can have respectful 'authentic' relations with others.

Heidegger has not gone into inter-personal relations in detail during his discussion of men's relation with each other.

It can be thus said that man living in this world recognizes the existence of others. Man cannot live alone. He needs others in order to fulfill his purposive goals. He co-exists not only for himself but for others too. In fact, man is essentially for the sake of others. He is inseparable from others since man belongs to the other men-selves and enhances their power and potentiality. Living with them, he identifies himself with them and the vice-versa. Man is ultimately the part of the social group and has a specific role in society. These social roles are defined not by the man but by the society itself.

CHAPTER XLII

DEATH AND ITS SIGNIFICANCE

Death occupies a central place in Martin Heidegger's exposition of human existence. Heidegger built up his impressive analysis of human existence in terms of care, with its three-fold structure possibility, reality and bondage. Death receives a key position in the existential analysis, as a fundamental ontology which is to provide a bridgehead into the question of being in general. The importance of the phenomenon of death extends into Heidegger's entire ontology. It indeed summons us back from the 'forgetting' of being and makes possible something like a confrontation with being.

Heidegger's own conviction is that death indeed enters into the structure of existence, for existence itself is a being-towards-death. Existence is dying, and death is present to us and, in a way, accessible to as, although we normally turn our attention away from it".[4] But to see how Heidegger leads into this understanding of the death, the following discussion on existential question of death will prove its worth.

Heidegger's analysis of the concept of death clarifies his distinction between authentic and inauthentic modes of human existence. Death is the innermost, irrelative and inevitable possibility of human existence. It is not a mere external event which terminates human existence at certain point of its history but is present in it; human existence from its very beginning, as structurally inherent to it, man's being-in-the-world, in due course of time, always leads to being towards death. The structural projection of human existence into the possibility of death renders all its other possibilities purely 'accidental' even while they exist as options. Death is, in this sense, the most important possibility of human existence which renders all its other possibilities and realities, contingent and transient.

It is death, or the threat of death, which makes authenticity possible. Authenticity is fundamentally facing and enduring death as one's own possibility. As possibility death lies in the future. Indeed, it lies at the very boundary of the future, closing it off. There is no further possibility beyond death. If death relates to the future as possibility, it also relates rather belongs to the reality of existence.

It is not something accidental or occasional in human existence, but something into which every existence is already thrown. To be born is already to be on the way to death, thus death is handed down to us along with our being as part of our heritage. We can take it over passively or we can actively appropriate it. Under no circumstances, however, can we get away from it. It is one certain factor in our existence.

For, Heidegger, death is the "end" of being whereby man becomes a "whole" and which makes life ultimately meaningful. Death is always someone's own death, and cannot be experienced vicariously. Heidegger maintains that no one can die for another, in the sense of taking the other's dying away from him and performing one's death for another. It is true, of course, that one man can go to his death for another, in the sense of, perhaps saving the other's life in a particular or definite situation, for a longer or shorter time. Such 'dying for other' however, can never signify that the other has thus had his death taken away in even the slightest degree. So, the successful attempt to reach an understanding of death by observing the death of others does at least lead to the recognition that death is un-transferable.

Heidegger further maintains that death is something that happens, usually to others, and thus does not concern me now; once it happens to me, it is too late for me to be concerned about anything that is involved in my own life because it is not a part of life.

Karl Jaspers on the other hand opines that death is a limitation inherent in the human situation. Human life in the world is riddled with the dreadful insecurity and irremediability (not remediable) of death as universal limit. Human existence learns to accept death as definitive. Karl Jaspers maintains that "death, so long as I am forgetting it or fleeing from it or merely taking note of it as the inevitable end, is just an empirical fact about an empirical object in the world of being-there. It is not constitutive of my life, and in so far as it is not, I am not living at the level of being oneself. My death is present; it is constitutive of my relation to the phenomena in which my whole life is manifested. It puts in question the sense in which, I am more than phenomena of my objective appearance. When I lose a friend by death with whom I lived in communication, the communication is struck but the presence of the lost one is not wholly destroyed, and by this my fidelity is maintained and continues to influence me. Thus, death is not a mere limit but a clue and a proof too".[5]

For Heidegger, death is man's ultimate possibility. It is the 'end (goal as well as termination) of a man's life. JP Sartre, on the other hand, although, clearly acknowledges the importance of death but denies its value as a goal of life. For Sartre, to be sure, death haunts me at the very heart of each of my projects as their inevitable reverse side. Death, for Sartre, is only a "boundary" of human life, and it is not a part of my life or part of my future or part of my possibilities at all. It is not my possibility but... the possibility that there are for me no longer any possibilities.... Death is not an obstacle to my projects... since death is beyond my subjectivity. There is no place for it in my subjectivity. There is no place for it in my subjectivity. For Sartre, death is not any sort of goal. Death is simply the end of his possibilities. It is not one of his possibilities.

For Heidegger, as for Soren Aabye Kierkegaard, death permeates all of life and it is, death which helps us in realizing our "true" selves. Death limits my possibilities by limiting my time. If I had infinite time, I could simply wait to do everything. With the knowledge of death, life becomes more urgent, and time becomes meaningful. Knowing of impending death gives meaning to life, a meaning which would not be had by an eternally living creature. It is my individual death which exposes the "nakedness" of my personal existence.

For Heidegger, as for Kierkegaard, the central problem of death is that we cannot understand it. Death reveals itself as something that knows no measures. Death is for us a simple "nothing".

Like Sartre and Heidegger, Kierkegaard recognizes the close relation of the individual's concept of death to his life of freedom. The anticipation of death makes a difference to all his decisions and transforms his life from inauthentic to authentic mode of existence. But Kierkegaard does not believe, like Heidegger and Sartre, the human existence is reduced to "nothingness" and becomes worthless in the face of its annihilation in death. Kierkegaard maintains that it acquires an infinite worth in as much as it participates in an inward God-relationship. The authentic life of the individual is not ultimately purposeless, as Sartre believes, but has the supreme purpose of entering into relationship with God.

Heidegger's own philosophy frankly accepts death, transience and finitude. Yet we have already seen enough of his, as well as, Kierkegaard's, Jaspers and Sartre's concept of death, to be impressed with the positive significance that it comes to have and that points us beyond any merely ritualistic interpretation. This positive significance appears to be two-fold.

1. In the first place, death becomes integrative rather than destructive. An authentic existence which resolutely anticipates death and understands all living to be also dying transcends the triviality of everyday existence and achieves meaning and unity. Death makes this possible. It becomes creative to selfhood.
2. In the second place, death or, to speak more accurately anxiety in the face of death, has the positive role of recalling man from forgetting of being, and awakening him to the wonder of being. It is the experience of nullity that brings awareness of being and prepares the way for that "primordial" thinking, a meditative thinking in which man receives the communication of being.

To conclude, the significance of death, for Heidegger, Sartre and Kierkegaard lies on the fact that death permeates all of life and gives meaning to the life. But for Sartre alone, death is not a goal in living. Death, for Heidegger, Sartre and Kierkegaard, helps man to transform his life from inauthentic to authentic existence but Sartre and Heidegger believe that death reduces human existence to "nothingness" and ultimately human existence becomes worthy if man enters in an inward relationship with God; whereas, for Karl Jaspers, death is a limitation inherent in the human situation.

Death is definitive and a hard fact of life though it is not constitutive of life. Death is personal experience of human being. Man has to accept death not as merely limit but as a clue and a proof very much present in the human situation. Finally, I reach to a conclusion that death is only a "boundary" rather limit of human life. Life comes to an end with death. Every man has a specific rather fixed span of life after that one has to meet death. Death is inevitable and imminent. No living being can escape death. Though death limits the life but it is not a hindrance to the activities of life. The fear of death in man will slow down the process of living.

Under this fear or awareness of death, man cannot work wholeheartedly and he will soon develop a sense of apathy towards his projects or goals and certainly it will affect the day-to-day living. And finally, man will be reduced to nothingness and his life after coming in contact with death comes to an end, becomes worthless and loses its importance.

HUMAN LIBERTY AND RESPONSIBILITY IN JEAN PAUL SARTRE'S PHILOSOPHY

CHAPTER XLIII

JEAN PAUL SARTRE (1905-1980): Brief Sketch and Introduction

JEAN PAUL SARTRE (1905-1980)

Jean-Paul Sartre

Sartre in March 1967

Born

Jean-Paul Charles Aymard Sartre, 21 June 1905

Paris, France

Died

15 April 1980 (aged 74), Paris, France

Education

École Normale Supérieure, University of aris[1] (B.A.; M.A., 1928)

Partner(s)

Simone de Beauvoir (1929–1980; his death)

Era

20th-century philosophy

Region

Western philosophy

School

Continental philosophy, existentialism, phenomenology, existential phenomenology,[2] hermeneutics,[2] Western Marxism, anarchism (late)

Main interests

Metaphysics, epistemology, ethics, consciousness, self-consciousness, literature, political philosophy, ontology

Notable ideas

Bad faith, "existence precedes essence", nothingness, "Hell is other people", situation, transcendence of the ego ("every positional consciousness of an object is a non-positional consciousness of itself"),[3][4] Sartrean terminology

Influences

- Kierkegaard,[2] de Beauvoir, Flaubert, Hegel, Heidegger, Husserl, Bergson, Kojève, Wahl, Bachelard, Darwin, Freud, Marx, Stekel, Merleau-Ponty, Nietzsche, Nizan, Levinas, Proust, Céline, Lefebvre,[5] Rousseau[6]

Influenced

- Aron, Camus, de Beauvoir, Fanon, Guevara, Laing, Goffman, Merleau-Ponty, Gorz, Lukács, Debord, Deleuze, Jeanson, Leibowitz, Lacan, Quito, Pinter, Rancière, Badiou, Bourdieu, van Fraassen, Butler

Courtesy -Wikipedia

JEAN PAUL SARTRE

Sartre was born in 1905 in France. He studied at the Ecole Normale Superieure in Paris. He went to Havre to teach at the Lycee. He taught Henri IV at the Lycee before going to the institute of François in Berlin in Germany in 1934. In 1935 he joined the staff of Lycee. From 1939-41, he was in the Army, and spent nine months as a prisoner of war in Germany. After his release, he was active in the resistance movement from 1941-44. Meanwhile in 1942 he resigned from the staff of the Lycee Condorcet to devote himself to his literary work. He edited the monthly review les temps Moderns since its inception in 1945. He died in 1980.

INTRODUCTION:

Several young and able French philosophers had found in the idea of Heidegger something fresh and significant which answers to their own feeling of anguish. The influence of Heidegger was directly felt in France, in a small circle of thinkers.

The philosophy of Jean Paul Sartre although containing much that is original with him; is linked in part to the philosophy of Heidegger and in part to that of Husserl. The latter leads him into a kind of idealism, which he may have derived from Heidegger. In common with Heidegger, Sartre has "the ontological concern", the need to study the idea of being, and also an emphasis on the idea of nothingness, though for Sartre this latter idea is often rendered in a sense more Hegelian than Heidegger.

Solomon Robert C. in "RATIONALISM TO EXISTENTIALISM" writes that "the watchwords of Sartre's philosophy from 1930s to the present have always been freedom and responsibility. The key to Sartre's thought is that every individual must choose and act for himself or herself. He insisted that we are always responsible for what we do, no matter what the ready excuses or the circumstances are. He always rejected "Marxism" which denied individual choice and responsibility and sought to replace individual responsibility with abstract forces over which society has no control.

Sartre himself confesses that "freedom is still the central concern of my entire philosophy, the freedom one has, the responsibility for what one is, even if there has been little that one could have about it. The responsibility for what one makes of what is made of one, perhaps, but no, I haven't changed my mind about freedom and responsibility.

CHAPTER XLIV

EXISTENCE IN-ITSELF AND FOR-ITSELF

Sartre's idea of human existence can well be found in his particular work i.e., "BEING AND NOTHINGNESS". In this book, Sartre characterizing modes of being holds that we must distinguish between being-in-itself, being-for-itself and being-for-others. These are the three modes of existence and the aim of "BEING AND NOTHINGNESS" as a whole can be said to be to explain the relation of the first to the second i.e., of being-in-itself to being-for-itself; and this is done partly by means of the third mode, i.e., being-for-others. Being-for-itself is identical with conscious being. Human beings are often referred to as for-itself.

Justus Streller, in the "TO FREEDOM CONDEMNED" writes that "the-for–itself and the-in-itself (a thing that is in-itself) are reunited by a synthetic connection which is nothing other than for-itself.
"The-for-itself", in fact, is nothing but the pure nihilism of the in-itself.

This nihilation, which determines the reality of for-itself, is enough to "cause a total upheaval to happen to the-in-itself. This upheaval is the world. It follows that the-for-itself is not independent. It is a non-substantial absolute Ian absolute because it uses its freedom to create itself). It depends on the–in-itself, it is for that reason always uncertain; its being is never established but always sought after.

It is only by making itself for-itself that being can aspire to be cause for-itself. This necessitates a break, with the identity of being of the in-itself, a withdrawal by being in relation to itself and the appearance of presence to self or consciousness. Hence being as a unity consisting of in-itself and for-itself is an ideal being, namely an in-itself grounded on and identical to a for-itself. It is therefore, the being which is its own cause. Everything happens therefore, the being which as if the in-itself and the for-itself were presented in a state of disintegration in relation to an ideal synthesis, a synthesis which has never occurred but which is always indicated and always possible.[1]

Since being-for-itself is identical with conscious being and that is nothing but human being itself. Therefore, it is very essential here to define that what the consciousness is? Sartre begins with the Husserlian dictum* that "all consciousness is consciousness of something", and also begins with the Cartesian doctrine that the existence of consciousness itself is known simply by virtue of its existence. This self-knowledge is not the defining characteristic of consciousness, for it ignores the 'pre-reflective consciousness, or 'pre-conscious intentionality'. The definition of 'consciousness' thus focuses on the intentionality of consciousness- it is always being directed towards an object. Thus, consciousness is nothing but this intentional activity; it is not an object itself or an object for-itself. Sartre characterizes this by "nothing" that consciousness is nothing. For Sartre, this leads to a distinction between two very different kinds of being- the being of objects for consciousness (being-in-themselves) and being of consciousness (being-for-itself), consciousness is said to be dependent on its objects for its own existence, and to avoid any postulation of consciousness as an object of some sort distinct from its objects, Sartre uses the expression 'consciousness (of)'; consciousness can be characterized as 'being for-itself' because its existence consists in its dependency on objects; and the possibility of explicit recognition of itself. Much of the characterization of being-for-itself, however, must be made in contrast to being-in-itself. Key to the distinction between the two kinds of being is the central important recognition that being-for-itself can never be an object of itself, "consciousness (of) itself. The nature of consciousness, of these two consciousness**, thus becomes a central problem for Sartre, and this problem may all be traced to the claim that consciousness cannot be an object for itself.

From the forgoing discussion, some central features of consciousness, as analyzed by Sartre, have become evident. Consciousness is necessarily consciousness (of) objects; consciousness is dependent on its objects. There is a pre-reflective consciousness which is not 'inhabited' by an ego; yet consciousness is necessarily self-consciousness. It is consciousness (of) being conscious (of) objects. Pre-reflective consciousness is not primarily a knowing consciousness but a 'living' experiencing consciousness; consciousness is not to be separated, even in logic from the world (and its objects) of which it is conscious.

In the "BEING AND NOTHINGNESS", the talk of reflective and pre-reflective consciousness also appears to be talk of two consciousnesses, one of which takes the other as an object. The distinction between reflective and pre-reflective consciousness cannot be a difference in self-consciousness. The fact that Sartre insists that self-knowledge and the ego appear only with reflective consciousness does not entail that self-consciousness is peculiar to reflection. On the contrary, Sartre insists that all consciousness, pre-reflective as well as reflective, is self-consciousness. The reflective cogito of Descartes has a pre-reflective analog. Only the reflective cogito constitutes self-knowledge (knowledge for Sartre is essentially reflective); but pre-reflective consciousness has its own (pre-reflective) cogito; it is also self-consciousness. Although reflective consciousness takes pre-reflective consciousness as its object in the (reflective) cogito, pre-reflective consciousness, according to Sartre, simply is self-consciousness; it does not take itself as an object. "Consciousness of self is not dual". Every conscious existence exists as consciousness of existing. We understand now why the first consciousness of consciousness is not positional; it is because it is one with the consciousness of which it is conscious".

"The self-consciousness we ought to consider not as a new consciousness, but as the only mode of existence which is possible for a consciousness of something".

Sartre does agree with Heidegger that there is a vital distinction between reflective and pre-reflective consciousness and a distinction between reflective self-knowledge (the Cartesian cogito) and pre-reflective self-consciousness; of course, consciousness can know and know itself. But it is in itself something other than knowledge turned back on 'itself'.

This complex and not sufficiently clear relationship between pre-reflective and reflective consciousness and self-consciousness lies at the very foundation of Sartre's philosophy. Specifically, his theory of nothingness and human freedom is based on a description of pre-reflective consciousness; which will be discussed later in this very chapter.

Summarizing, it can be said that Sartre's "being-for-itself" is helplessly pitched against the "being-in-itself" in which it endlessly struggles to realize itself but is incapable of doing so securely because of its own tendency towards separation and the corresponding transiency of its own realization in the "being-in-itself". The "being-for-itself" hence meets with repeated disappointments and frustration, is the last word in Sartre's philosophy, which leaves no room for the possibility of transcending the conflict.

---

*Edmund Husserl was the teacher of Martin Heidegger. Husserl in his philosophical teaching had shown the concern for philosophical efforts. Husserl helped his pupil, Martin Heidegger, in understanding his particular brand of phenomenology neglects individual existence. Husserl influenced Sartre too. Husserl pointed out in one of his central 'discoveries' that cogito always finds itself confronting an object (cogitation). Husserl interpreted the cogitation or objects confronting the cogito or 'reduced' or 'bracketed' objects of consciousness. The Cartesian doctrine concerns the 'self-evidence' of the cogito and dubitable existence of 'the world' (From Rationalism of Existentialism- Solomon Robert C. P.184-185, 213).

**In the "TRANSCENDENCE OF THE EGO", it often sounds as if there are literally two consciousnesses being described, for example, when Sartre says that "my reflecting (reflective) consciousness does not take itself for an object when I reflect the cogito. What it affirms concerns the reflected (pre-reflective) consciousness".

CHAPTER XLV

NOTHINGNESS AND NIHILATION

The concept of nothing and nothingness have been recurrent in my discussions of Heidegger. Now the same will be discussed for Sartre, in this chapter. The phenomenological conceptions of nothing and nothingness are not commonsense conceptions. For Sartre, consciousness is nothing. This means that consciousness is not an object.

Closely tied to the concepts of nothing and nothingness is the concept of nihilation. Nihilation is an activity of consciousness and is responsible for the existence of nothingness * in the world. Furthermore, consciousness itself is said to be nothingness and it is responsible for producing nothingness.

In the "BEING AND NOTHINGNESS", we find that it is (pre-reflective) consciousness itself which is responsible for nihilation. Nothingness is a component of our experience in the world. Nothingness and nihilation spread through all of human conscious activities specially freedom and responsibility, and ultimately, distinguish man from all other beings. It is through nihilation and nothingness that human freedom is introduced into Sartre's phenomenology.

Let us first examine the claim that nothingness is an object of our experience "in the world". Common sense would seem to claim that we never see nothing; but always see something. Our consciousness of world is a consciousness of real objects in the world. Of course, consciousness of imagined objects then becomes a serious problem. If we ask, do we only see something? Sartre's answer is that we do not just see "something", but, even in perception, see nothings. In other words of saying, we are not only conscious of the presence of objects in our world; we are also conscious of their absence. For example, when I am expecting a friend to drop in my house, or waiting for a phone call, I am not only conscious of the presence of the door, the telephone, and the other objects around me, I am primarily aware, of the lack of the knock of the door and the failure of the telephone to ring. Nothingness, the lack of absence of something rather than the presence of something, is definitive of my situation.

Sartre calls such experiences as experiences of our environment as inhabited by nothingness. With regard to negation and the experience of nothingness, Sartre gives us a reasonably clear picture of 'experience of nothingness'. Nothingness is experienced in experience of absence of objects, and, as an object of experience, nothingness is itself a sort of being. **

Being does not proceed from nothingness, on the contrary, nothingness is logically subsequent to being; nothingness posits being in order to deny it. The total disappearance of being would not be the advent of the reign of non-being, but on the contrary the concomitant disappearance of nothingness.

Non-being is forever there, in us and outside us. Being is haunted by non-being, but non-being appears only where being might be expected. In other words, non-being can appear only if it has previously been posited as a possibility. Non-being does not come to things through a negative judgment; it is the negative judgment, on the contrary, which is conditioned and supported by non-being. Nothingness must be given if there is to be negation and negative judgments. There must be negation in order for us to be able to ask questions, and especially to question being. But nothingness cannot be produced by being for being is wholly positive. Nothingness must be given inside being-in the heart of being like an internal parasite. Nothingness does not nihilate, as Heidegger supposes, for in order to do this, it would have to possess being. It does not have its own being. It has only a borrowed being. Nothingness is not in a position to nihilate itself; nothingness is nihilated.

Nihilation can be accomplished only by an existent whose being encloses the nothingness of being. The being by which nothingness comes to the world must be its own nothingness. To put it in other words, this being can be only man, for only man can ask questions and confront negativities.

Every destructible, fragile existent carries within its being "a definite possibility of non-being". The revelation of this possibility is affected through man. An object becomes precious or fragile when posits as fragile and takes measure to keep it from being destroyed.[2]

Summarizing, it can be said that man is the only being who performs acts consciously. Every conscious act is an act with intention. Thus, every intentional conscious act is an act with intention. Thus, every intentional conscious act involves expectation and in turn; an act of nihilation. In other words, it can be said that every act of consciousness includes within the "possibility of meaningless" i.e., the consciousness. All acts of nihilation are involved in every conscious act and that consequently the experience of nothingness is (at least potentially) involved in every human experience.

As said, every human experience involved nothingness and every consciousness is filled up with expectations, expectation that can at any time be thwarted, and human existence is thereby something essentially open to frustration, disappointment, despair, all of which are experience of nothingness involving acts of nihilation. Frustration, for example, is the result of non-fulfilled expectation, the experience of not doing or not having what one wants. Man (Being-for-itself) is all possibilities and all expectations. Being-in-itself cannot be from the world. Man (being-for-itself) is constantly threatened by nothingness, for its very nature is to project possibilities and to expect things from the world. And at the same time man also wishes to remain free, to continue to hope and plan for the future, to expect things of the future.

---

*The central concern of "Being and Nothingness", is the mode of existence of the conscious subject. As conscious subjects capable of sensing, perceiving, emoting, remembering, imagining, thinking, judging, choosing and deciding, we exist in a wholly different way from the things of which we are conscious. What is essential to this kind of existence is that it is always being projected beyond itself, always in a process of being realized and being renewed. Conscious subjects, are always in a state of something other than they are, they are what they are not yet. This state of not-being-yet and this openness to further possibilities; which is an essential feature of consciousness. (The existentialist and JP Sartre, Max Charles Worth, P. 27)

**It is not correct, however to say that "being" and "nothingness", are two kinds of being on equal ontological footing. Hegel, for example, had argued that "being and non-being are logically contemporary. And Heidegger at one time in the "WHAT IS METAPHYSICS", had similarly defended an ontological independent nothing. Sartre insists that "non-being exists only on the surface of being". (From "Rationalism to Existentialism", Solomon Robert C. P. 268)

CHAPTER XLVI

HUMAN LIBERTY

There is no concept more central to 'existentialist' thought than the concept of 'freedom'. Kierkegaard insisted that human being, subjectivity, and freedom were equivalent; Heidegger similarly interprets 'Dasein' as freedom. Sartre makes the concept of freedom the defining 'structure' of for-itself or human consciousness.

Freedom is also a key concept in the works of many obviously, not-existentialist thinkers, for example, Kant, Hegel and Husserl. The doctrine that man is essentially free does not suffice to distinguish those philosophies which are peculiarly 'existentialist'.

Perhaps there is no single doctrine of human freedom which is common to Sartre and other existentialist philosophers. However, certain peculiarly existentialist themes recur in their various philosophies; the doctrine that there is no human nature or 'essence', that man makes himself; and the thesis that human freedom entails not only freedom from causal determination but a freedom from rational moral, divine, or 'naturalistic' imposition of values or goals. Both theses clearly distinguish the existentialist from non-existentialist thinkers like Kant, Hegel and Husserl, who argued that human values and goals could be objectively or rationally validated. Existentialist freedom is both freedoms from causal determination and from rational coercion.

Before discussing Sartre's views on human freedom in detail, the views put forward by Kierkegaard and Heidegger on human freedom is given to have a distinction among them.

Kierkegaard's conception of human freedom is based on his faith in God and his faith in man's inherent capacity to enter into bonds of commitment to God. Life lived in devotion to God and in pursuit of moral life is the ethico-religious stage of human existence as distinguished from its purely aesthetic stage. The choice between these levels of human existence is an existential choice which presents itself to each man as an either/or. Man, himself is involved in making choice and choice he makes decides the levels of his existence. The either/or expresses the existential relation between the ethico-religious and the aesthetic level of existence. Either he chooses the ethico level of existence, and enters upon an inward commitment to

God and thereby realizes that he is an 'existing' individual, or he completely loses himself in objective pleasures or theoretical speculations and thereby forgets that he is an 'existing' individual. In this 'existential' choice man does not chose everything outside himself but chose himself, either to exist as a unique individual or not to exist. The existential choice essentially connotes the reality of the act of choice rather than the object of choice.

In basing the life of freedom on faith in God, Kierkegaard differs from Sartre and Heidegger. For Sartre and Heidegger, freedom of human existence implies the life of man oriented towards the realization of one's own inherent potentiality of being through personal choice; theirs is an earth-bound conception of freedom, and 'transcendence'. It means for them man's passing from the present state of his being-in-the-world to its future states by exercising his own personal decision in the process. Both Sartre and Heidegger propound a philosophy of human finiteness and limit the significance of the life of freedom to an existence which is temporal and finite. But Kierkegaard regards the self as a synthesis of the future and the finite and infinite, the temporal and the eternal, and conceives the life of freedom as an unfolding of its capacity for infinite love and eternal happiness by transcending one's egocentric limitations. The life of freedom is oriented towards an inward personal relationship with God, who is transcendent and eternal, and not towards the realization of one's worldly possibilities.

Heidegger's concept of freedom comes to light in his distinction between the authentic and the inauthentic modes of human existence. Man's freedom consists in the exercise of personal choice so as to cultivate, develop and realize his own inherent potentiality-of-being and this freedom is 'lost' when subordinates all his decision and actions to the approval of public opinion. According to Heidegger, man becomes free to the extent that be disentangles himself from the inauthentic mode of human existence characterized by his 'fallenness' and lostness; in the publicness of the 'thy-self' and resolve, to live an authentic mode of human existence by orienting his life towards realization of his potentiality-of-being. Freedom from the 'fallenness' or 'lostness' into the publicness of the 'they-self' as one like many is the measure of one's freedom of authentic being oneself. This is Heidegger's concept of freedom based on his distinction between the authentic and the inauthentic modes of human existence.

Like Sartre, Heidegger also believes that freedom in the sense of inherent 'nothingness' of human existence is basically the ontological 'truth' of human existence and that the practice of this 'truth' in man's authentic existence manifests itself as his ethical or moral life. For both, Heidegger and Sartre, to be true to one's existence is also to be ethical and moral.

Sartre's concept of freedom is closely related with his concept of 'nothingness'; the identification of human existence with its inherent 'nothingness' resulting in the human self who is regarded as the requisite condition of human freedom. It is because the human self is inherently 'nothing' countless and is 'free' to express itself in the various decisions and actions, it 'separates' itself from them and retains its freedom for its further self-expression without being lost into one of its self-expressions. Man becomes aware of his freedom when he becomes aware of his 'inherent' nothingness and refuses to identify himself with any of his achievement or realization.

Freedom pertains to the process of self-expression of the projective consciousness (nothingness) in being-in-itself and as such is essentially bound up with its activity. To be 'free' is to act and in the absence of activity there can be no freedom, but there can be no absence of activity since even to abstain from activity is itself an act and hence express freedom.

Man is hence condemned to be free in the sense that all his acts (including the deliberate act of his subordination of freedom to an external authority and an act of suicide) are expressions of his freedom of choice. Both authentic and inauthentic modes of existence are grounded in man's inherent freedom. *

Sartre's absolute freedom is not the exaggerated popular claim that 'a man can do anything he wants to do'. But rather than man is always free within his situation to confer significance upon that situation. Absolute freedom is freedom of choice, freedom of intention, or freedom of significance (these are ultimately equivalent) and not freedom of success in action. Freedom is limited by one's situation and freedom are absolutely only within these limitations. "Our freedom does not destroy our situation, but gears itself to it".

Making a distinction between freedom and arbitrariness, it can be said that 'to be free' does not mean 'to obtain what one has wished' but rather 'by oneself to determine oneself to wish' (in the broad sense of choosing). In other words, success is not important to freedom.

There is no denial that external circumstances may thwart action or cause actions to fumble, but Sartre does maintain that all such 'external circumstances' are such only in view of the goals, we seek to achieve;

"human reality everywhere encounters resistance and obstacles which it has not created, but these resistance and obstacles have meaning only in and through the free choicc which human reality is".

Sartre maintains that my choice is free and I am responsible for it only as far as that choice is made in that situation. Sartre also allows those men are not always responsible for their actions such as the success of their actions. Sartre allows no leniency with regard to responsibility for one's intentions and one's choices; for the freedom to intend and the freedom to choose is absolute.

Human freedom is not a part of human existence; it precedes human existence and makes it possible. The freedom of man cannot be separated from the being of man. It is the being of man's consciousness. It is not a human attribute but it is the raw material of my beings. I owe my being to freedom. Freedom is the basis for all human activity. To act is to modify the shape of the world. Human activity is basically intentional, goal oriented. The action necessarily implies that something will be created which has not previously existed, it implies a lack or a negatively something not yet realized.

To conclude it can be said that there is no action without a cause. An action without cause would lack an intentional structure. It would be not an action but a reaction. Thus, it can be empathetically said that there can be no act without a cause but this does not mean that the motive is the cause of the act. It is rather an integrating component; motive, act and goal constitute a unity which appears as a single upsurge, this upsurge is one with freedom. Freedom makes itself an act, and we ordinarily attain it across the act which it organizes with the cause, motives and ends which the act implies.

Having rejected the world of ideas or essence, and analogous concepts, Sartre draws the logical conclusion from his position. The choice of our ends is also absolutely free; it is made without any basis. It is founded on no reason for the good reason that all reasons, come into the world by free choice; that is to say that everyone chooses freely the norms of truth, beauty and goodness. We are free, therefore, absolutely. The norms behind our judgment of value, the ultimate motives of our decisions, are free. Only we must not conceive these motives and norms as objects of thoughts. The profound choice that determines our decisions for all our lives is bound to be one and the same as the consciousness that we have of ourselves.

To summarize, it can be said that 'a free being is one who makes choices relating to his past in the context of his future and who does not let himself be determined by the present". He makes his essence known by his end (toward which he projects himself from the other side of the world which he transcends); thus, the fundamental act of freedom becomes "a choice of myself in the world", and at the same times "a discovery of the world". And after this discovery, human beings continue to exist in this very world. In so far as human beings continue to exist, they continue to choose their ends, for freedom is the essence of human beings' existence. On the occasion of any particular choice, they can call in question their former choice. It follows that any decision taken in conformity with it may be regarded as a renewal of that choice. Thus, human beings have the right to consider all their voluntary acts as free. To choose is to live; every act which is not a rigid consequence of what human beings are may be called free.

It follows that liberty is not the prerogative only of my voluntary acts. My emotions and passions, which also depend on what I am, are equally free; they are, like volitions, certain subjective attitudes by which we attempt to attain the ends laid down by our original liberty; my fear is free, and is a manifestation of my freedom. * [*Ibid, PP 520, 521]

Everything in our psychological life is therefore free. But does that not amount to the same thing as saying that there is no liberty? If everything is free in our inner life, it is because the word freedom is not understood by Sartre in the sense usually intended by philosophers, and even by ordinary people. There can be no freedom except in an act determined by motives, and common sense does not regard as free an act carried out under the stress of a blind urge. How to act freely consists, in setting up without a motive and even without being aware of it. In fact, the free, acts are eminently rational; but for Sartre, it is absurd; it is absurd because it is beyond all reasons. ** . It is related to instinctive, and not to rational, actively.[3]

Sartre, further, maintains that "in love, it is the liberty of the other that separates the other from me and constitutes me as an object revealing my outside to the other. In loving, I demand that one I love shall exist solely to choose me as an object, and this be the origin of my existence for another; it is this alone that gives me an existence.[4]

I cannot escape being the object of another free existence which limits my liberty, and I cannot live the situation and characteristics attributed to me by the other, but I can at least will this entire situation, to be limited by the freedom of the other; and this brings the external limit inside my situation under my choice. I beyond my situation, and that this involves my being there in the middle of the world for someone else, and by willing that situation and reacting to it in the circumstances of my particular case I bring it into my situation under my liberty, although it remains unrealized.

Thus, for Sartre, the true limit of his freedom lies purely and simply in the very fact that another apprehends him as the other-as-object and in that second corollary fact that his situation ceases for the other to be a situation and becomes an objective form in which he exists as an objective structure. Freedom is total and indefinite but it does not mean that it has no limits but that it never encounters them.[5]

Heidegger says that "death is a pure fact, like birth; I am not 'free in order to die' but 'a free being who dies', I chose to assume my death as the inconceivable limit of my subjectivity, as I choose to be; liberty limited by the fact of the liberty of another. In neither case do I encounter this limit as a fetter upon my liberty. This is Sartre's account of human freedom.[6]

---

*Man is free within a given situation, then he will easily grasp that this freedom may be defined as authentic or as inauthentic according to the choice it makes of itself within the situation when it arises. Authenticity, it goes without saying, consists in assuming a lucid and true awareness of the situation, in accepting the responsibilities and risks incurred in that situation and in maintaining it in the moment of pride or of humiliation, and sometimes in the moment of abhorrence and hatred. There is no doubt that authenticity requires great courage, and something more than courage; when the authentic man becomes aware or if life is worth living, but rather he asks if he wants to live and under what condition. If there is no God, man bears the responsibility for the world. (Portrait of the Anti-Semite, JP Sartre, P.75)

**Ibid, PP 559

CHAPTER XLVII

HUMAN POSSIBILITIES

The human possibilities as understood by JP Sartre will be discussed here. The essential characteristic of the human being (for-it-self) is that it is a lack. It needs something to complete. In explaining what Sartre means by the lack* which is the characteristic of consciousness, Sartre makes use of the concept of the "possible". Sartre says, consciousness lacks something for something else..."as the broken disc of the moon lacks that which would be necessary to complete it, and transform it into a full moon". What is lacked by a conscious being is 'the confidence of himself with himself'. That is to say the for-itself seeks for the self-identity or the completeness which is the characteristic of a different mode of being, namely Being-in-itself; what I ceaselessly aim towards, is myself, that which am not, my own possibilities.

Sartre takes trouble to explain what he means by 'the possible', but nevertheless it is difficult to be quite sure what he means. He wishes to say that the possibility of a thing actually belongs to it, as properties. When we say that it may possibly rain, we do not simply mean that we can conceive either of its raining or of its not raining, without logical contradiction. We mean more than this; we are referring, he says, to come actual feature of the clouds. "The possible is a concrete property of already existing realities". In order for the rain to be possible there must be clouds in the sky.

Now relating possibility with human beings, Sartre insists that unless there were conscious beings in the world there would be no such thing as possibilities. The mere properties of physical objects, though they are necessary before we can talk of possibilities, are not by themselves sufficient to entitle us to do so. We need also to see the world as organized in a certain way to bring to bear. For instance, our inductively acquired knowledge of the world to judge what categories of things we are dealing with before we can see something as possible. Thus, to say of being-for-itself or consciousness that it strives all the time towards own possibilities is to say that it is self-awareness, for without the awareness and the organizing nature of a mind thinking of possibilities there would be no possibilities to strive towards forward.

Consciousness according to Sartre is always referring forward, away from a more momentary awareness of what is truc now. Sartre, for example, says "consciousness of reading ins not consciousness of reading this letter or this word or this sentence or even this paragraph; it is consciousness of residing this book, which refers me to all the pages still unread, to all the pages already read, which by definition detaches consciousness from itself; a consciousness which was conscious only of what it would be obliged to spell out every word. So, the lack which is at the heart of consciousness is a lack which completed possibilities; and it must always remain unsatisfied as long as a being is conscious.[7]

Being-for-itself projects various possibilities for itself and places a value on these different alternatives. Value is "the beyond and of transcendence. Transcendence is to be understood not as a detached consideration of possible course of section, but as a concerned (even 'anguished') searched for a value for these imminent possibilities.

The characterization of the transcendence of the for-it-self as the projection of possibilities and the "positing of values" leads us an important step closer to an understanding of Sartre's doctrine of freedom and its connection with the analysis of nothingness. Being-for-itself also is "being-for-values", and both is and is not its own possibilities.

Here we notice that how this network of key concepts inter-relations to form our concept of "human reality". Man is free to act as he chooses and he chooses according to his evaluations of various possible states of affairs-more accurately, possible situations for him and he does so by virtues of the fact that consciousness is really nothingness. This nothingness, however, as nihilation, forbidden as it sounds, is in turn analyzed in terms of acts of nihilation. The nothingness of consciousness is the ability to "wrench oneself away" from the real world and envision and evaluate possibilities for modifying that world.

Sartre's analysis of desire * is analyzed in terms of a lack and we notice that conscious acts of nihilation necessarily turn to consciousness itself. "For-itself cannot sustain nihilation without determining itself a lack of being".

It is this notice of a 'lack of being'. In turn, which forms the basis of the analysis of desire and, which in turn, forms the basis of the analysis of all human transcendence;" of all internal negations, the one which penetrates most deeply into being...this negation is lack. It appears in the world only with the upsurge of human reality. It is only in the human world that there can be lacks.

Sartre says that the realization of the possibility of negation is a function not only of our judgments about the world, but of our attitudes to the world before we make any judgments whatever, for instance, the concept of negation enters into expectation, which may be pre-verbal and is essentially such that it may be disappointed. In the same sort of way, we may intuitively apprehend, the absence of things as well as their presence.

It is our expectation and presuppositions which produce such concepts as 'absence'. But, granted that this is so, we can perceive absence as clearly as we can perceive presence. There is no question, then, but that negation enters into out awareness of the world, and therefore into our awareness of ourselves, at a very early, pre-rational level.

Being-in-itself is 'complete' or fulfilled and has no possibilities, that is, sees no possibilities for itself and has no expectations. Being-for-itself, on the contrary is all possibilities and all expectations. Being-in-itself cannot be frustrated or disappointed because it expects nothing from the world. Being-for-itself is constantly threatened by nothingness, for its very nature is to project possibilities, to expect things from the world. To be God would be to project infinite possibilities and have infinite expectations for oneself, but it would also be complete or fulfilled and beyond the possibility of disappointment. In his search to escape frustration and nothingness in general, man seeks to be in-itself, complete and determined so that his future is not an open question, a series of possibilities and expectations many of which will be frustrated. But it is death, the end of one's possibilities, the end of one's transcendence and thus marks the point at which we can finally treat a man as a being-in-itself, because every moment we are alive, offers us new choices and new possibilities. Being-in-itself is pure "coincidence with itself", but by virtue of this coincidence with itself it cannot be conscious of this; the life of a man is essentially dissatisfied and unfulfilled. Only his death satisfies and fulfills his, but not necessarily according to his own projects and goals for himself. (The satisfaction of death lies solely in man's final 'coincidence with himself' and not in the fulfillment of any particular ideal for himself.

For Heidegger, death is man's ultimate possibility. I am the "and" (goal as well as terminations) of a man's life. Sartre clearly acknowledges the importance of death but denies its value as a goal in living. To be sure, "Death haunts me at the very heart of each of my projects as their inevitable reverse side". Death is only a "boundary" of human life, and it is not part of my life or part of my future or part of my possibilities at all. It is not "my possibilities but......the possibility that there are for me no longer any possibilities. Death is not an obstacle to my projects.... since death is always beyond my subjectivity. There is no place for it in my subjectivity". I may and probably must live with the knowledge that I am going to die, but I need not, Sartre at least implies that I ought not to take my death as any sort of goal. Death is simply the end of my possibilities; it is not one of my possibilities.[8]

According to Sartre, "Desire is the link between mere consciousnesses of the world and self-consciousness of the world". Further he writes that desire is not a 'psychic state or a physical force' nor is it a fact about the world. Our desires are recognitions of a certain lack (a failing, dissatisfaction, nothingness) in the world, but it is only our expectations of what the world ought to be like which allows us to perceive such lacks.

Summarizing, it can be said that possibilities for Sartre is a sort of a "lack". Human beings strive all along their lives to fill this gap or complete this lack and become whole and identify themselves with their true selves. The existence of desire also proves the human reality as a lack. Because unless human beings feel them-selves complete, they will continue to strive towards this completeness. They have desires which are nothing but their expectations to bring the necessary changes in the world according to their needs. Thus, man strives to surpass himself from his present state to transcendence mode of existence which is again nothing nut a desire of human being to actualize his possibilities. In this process of realizing his possibilities, he embraces death which is nothing but the end of all possibilities. Death brings an end to the transcendence. With their death, man must feel satisfied and his all-desires possibilities fulfilled. But death should not be taken as a goal of human life to satisfy his desires and fulfill his expectations; since death is the termination of human life. Thus, all human possibilities come to stand still with the coming of death and human life comes to a grinding halt.

---

*Sartre explaining lack says that "human reality by which lack appears in the world must itself be a lack......The existence of desire as a human fact is sufficient to prove that human reality is a lack". Sartre further says that lack is the being of being-in-itself. In other words, consciousness is indeterminate, it lacks a fixed nature, and all desire is directed towards making itself determinate. This determinacy towards which being-for-itself strives is the self or ego; all possibilities, desires, specifically are directed towards this self; "The possible is something which for-itself lacks in order to be itself". (From "Rationalism to Existentialism", Solomon Robert C. P. 276)

CHAPTER XLVIII

HUMAN RESPONSIBILITY

Here we will discuss the human responsibility as understood by Sartre. An attempt will be made to co-relate the terms, "Freedom and Responsibility'.

Freedom and responsibility are co-relative terms, in the strict sense that they imply each other. If and in as much as the for-it-self is free, it must be responsible; the extent of its responsibility is precisely that of its freedom. The reason for this relationship of mutual implication between freedom and responsibility lies in the fact that each is conceivable as an alternative description of consciousness itself. "Responsibility" means "consciousness as authorship" and that "freedom" signifies "consciousness" as nihilating choice.

As said, human freedom involves responsibility; to be in a situation which is the being of human presence in the world, is to be responsible for one's manner of being; I am inescapably responsible because my ends which are mine alone determine my situation. Man has a freedom within a given situation"; and this freedom may be defined as authentic or as inauthentic mode of human existence. According to the choice it makes of itself within the situation when it arises.

Authenticity consists in assuming a lucid and true awareness of the situation, in accepting the responsibilities and risk incurred in that situation and in maintaining 'it in the moment of pride or of humiliation, and sometimes even in the moment of abhorrence and hatred. When the authentic man becomes aware of his freedom, it is foolish to ask if his life is worth living. Man lives in this very world and bears the responsibility for the world. No one can say whether or not man's existence has any importance. *

Man being condemned to be free carries the weight of the world on his shoulders; he is responsible for the world and for himself as a way of being. We are taking the world "Responsibility" in its ordinary sense as "consciousness (of) being the incontestable author of an event or of an object". In this sense the responsibility of the for-it-self is overwhelming since he is the one by whom it happens that there is a world; since he is also the one who makes himself be.

The authorship concept underscores what recent responsibility theorists call “imputability’. The imputed situation is held to be dependent on a subject in a significant manner. But in Sartre’s usage, imputability is not the result of causing something (causality being limited to natural processes, which Sartre tends to ignore); rather, it is a function of “choice” and of various more specific form of action. Consequently, the range of imputability is simple staggering. It extends to all that I am or do, to the meaning of what others do, and indeed to the very fact that “there is” a world at all. Yet this claim is not so astounding when read in light of his theory of consciousness-freedom as world-constituting.

There is another dimension to “responsibility”, namely accountability or liability for praise or blame, which might seem to be excluded by Sartre’s authorship use. Imputability and accountability, no doubt, are distinct uses of “responsibility” and can be separated as, for example, when a parent is held responsible (accountable) for the effects of his child’s actions (imputability).

But it is especially by choosing “authorship” in place of causality that Sartre reverses a broadly moral sense for the term “responsibility”. This important claim follows from at least four considerations. **First**, authorship is properly human relationship; it does not obtain among physical or apparently even among merely biological entities. **Second**, as a phenomenon of the pre-reflective cogito, basic responsibility presupposes ontological freedom and original choice. **Third**, it is by that same token value-constituting. Whatever we originate is always done under the protection of our fundamental project which, in turn, is our way of choosing our ideal self. And this choice of self is choice of an image of what we believe every person should be. **Finally**, responsibility is broadly moral because it is constitutive of personhood along with selfness and world.

I refer to authorship responsibility as “broadly” moral to distinguish it from specific ethical judgments which will be called on to justify at the everyday level. Thus, I can urge to “assume” responsibility for a state of affairs by my conduct in the world precisely I am responsible in the ontological sense.

To summarize, by speaking of “incontestable” authorship, Sartre is appealing to the well-known existentialist absence of excuses. “The peculiar character of human reality is that it is without excuses”. ** But Sartre’s incontestable means that responsibility can never allow excuses and hence that it cannot admit of degrees. He occasionally refers to this responsibility as absolute. ***

Furthermore, this absolute responsibility is not resignation; it is simply the logical requirement of the consciousness of our freedom. What happens to me happens through me, and I can neither affect myself with it nor revolt against it nor resign myself to it. Moreover, everything which happens to me is mine. The most terrible situation of war, the worst tortures do not create nonhuman state of things; there is no non-human situation. It is only through fear, flight, and recourse to magical types of conduct that I shall decide on the non-human, but this decision is human, and I shall carry the entire responsibility for it, but in addition the situation in because it is the image of my free choice of myself, and everything which it presents to me is mine in that this represents me and symbolizes me. Since man creates himself; his responsibility is "total". But is total responsibility possible? It is hardly convincing that a single individual decides for the "entire race", "for all" because each single individual has to decide for himself. Our acts may be wrong or outrageous that many endanger many-or-even a whole society- "that is the meaning of the world and the place of man in the universe". [9] Man's responsibility extends far beyond what, from a common-sense point of view, he could have chosen freely. Nothing eludes it. It includes not only the inner, personal activity, but also external events. I am responsible for everything, "as deeply responsible for the war (here Sartre refers to Second World War) as if I had declared it myself. Sartre assumed the responsibility for all that happened in the world. ****

The responsibility of the for-it-self (human being) extends to the entire world as a peopled-world. It is precisely thus that the for-it-self apprehends itself in anguish; that is, as a being which is neither the foundation of its own being nor of the other's being nor of the in-itself which form the world, but a being which is compelled to decide the meaning of being-within it and everywhere outside of it. The one who realizes in anguish his condition as being thrown into a responsibility which extends to his very abandonment has no longer either remorse or regret or excuses; he is no longer anything but a freedom which perfectly reveals itself and whose being resides in this very revelation. But, most of the time we flee anguish in bad faith. [10] *****

To summarize, it can be said that freedom and responsibility are interrelated terms. Freedom implies responsibility. Man can be held responsible for his acts only. He cannot be held responsible for the actions he did not do. A man is responsible for his actions only because in acting he acts in his own, unique situation and also involves the interests of his fellow beings living in the society. Sartre is right in stressing the responsibility for others even in solitary decisions but he is wrong in making men responsible for the actions, they are not involved at all. Sartre is wrong in overloading the men with total responsibility. Under no circumstances, man could be held responsible for the acts he did not do, for the situations he did not create. Therefore, one single individual cannot be held responsible for the happenings in the world. Sartre is wrong in holding himself responsible for the Second World War which broken out in 1939. Only he could be held responsible for the individual decisions or steps (if any) connected with the declaration of the Second World War.

To conclude, it can be said that individual must assume responsibility for his society, for his fellow beings and must have a duty to work for the improvement of society and wellbeing of his fellow men.

----

*French Existentialist, Kingston Fredrick Temple P 177

** Refers BEING AND NOTHINGNESS, JP SARTRE, P. 555

*** Refers BEING AND NOTHINGNESS, JP SARTRE, P. 554

**** I am responsible for everything, in fact, except for my very responsibility, for I am not the foundation of my being. Therefore, everything takes place as if I were compelled to be responsible. I am abandoned in the world. And I find myself suddenly alone and without help, engaged in a world for which I bear the whole responsibility without being able, whatever I do, to tear myself away from the responsibility for an instant. I am responsible for my very desire of fleeing responsibilities. (BEING AND NOTHINGNESS, JP SARTRE, P. 500)

*****Refers BEING AND NOTHINGNESS, JP SARTRE, P. 556

CHAPTER XLIX

COMPARATIVE STUDY OF SARTRE'S FORMER AND LATER THOUGHTS ON HUMAN LIBERTY

Jean Paul Sartre's theory of human freedom has undergone some 'radical changes" during nineteen sixties.

To begin with, Sartre emphatically declares that freedom is not a synonym for power. To be free does not mean that one can do whatever one wants to do. Things in the world and the actions of other people offer resistance. But obstacles do not prevent freedom; they are what make freedom possible, if wish were synonyms with fulfillment, then there would be no distinction between dream and reality. Moreover, a freedom without material or logical limitation would be infinite; and since man himself is finite, it would no longer be a human freedom. If freedom is to be meaningful at all; it must be freedom to choose, and choices demand alternative possibilities which limit each other. The resistance of the world outside us is the material out of which freedom forms its projects. Sartre goes into infinite detail to show that whatever may be his reality (his factual limits of time, space physical strength, and external events about him); it is he who determines its significance, its meaning for him, and its place in his life. *

Sartre discusses at some length the "resistance and obstacles" which human beings encounter but cannot overcome except by deciding on different purposes in relation to those brute givens. Thus, for example, "the rock appears to me in the light of a projected scaling... what my freedom, cannot determine, is, whether the rock "to be scaled" or will not lead itself to scaling". ** There is freedom only in a situation. Sartre insists, this situation includes a number of objective physical (gifts) which would prevent out being free to do as we chose; place, body, past, and positions are among these. *** None of these, however, poses a limit to human freedom, according to Sartre's earlier theory the point is that freedom to do is not what Sartre meant at that time by freedom. On the other hand, Sartre did not mean freedom-to-do in the irrational manner required by an indeterminist position. He explicitly rejected an indeterminist position, in part because it renders the particular action "absurd". **** He spells out the point that when he speaks of freedom, he does not mean a "capricious, unlawful gratuitous and incomprehensible contingency. ***** In opposition to the indeterminist position, Sartre claims that "to speak of an act without a cause is to speak of an act which would lack the intentional structure of every act. ******

For Sartre, our chosen ends operate as a kind of final cause. The indeterminist position would not be relevant to moral decision making since it would view action as occurring by chance what is needed; however, is an agent who is responsible for what is, causes his own acts.

His theory of freedom does not concern a freedom to do as we choose either in a contra causal sense or in the sense that human beings are omnipotent.

Sartre's theory of freedom is connected with the choice of an ideal self, but he makes it clear that "success is not important to freedom" #, that is, one is no less free in one's choice of self if one has not fully realized the ideal self. When he says "Man is a useless passion"; Sartre is insisting that the ideal self is in fact unrealizable. ##

A number of aspects of the person are objectively given and are not, as such, subject to our choice, for instance race, sex, class, nationality physiological structure. It is not a matter of choice that I am crippled but it is a matter of choice whether I make my disability an excuse for failure or something to be proud of, or a humiliation. ###

Sartre thinks we are free to choose ourselves in the sense of choosing the self we want to be. But in other sense we are not in the least free to choose, what we are one must distinguish between those senses. Here it should be added that he does not always make these distinctions explicit and that he sometimes misleadingly speaks as if freedom were "total".

We have seen that Sartre's earlier theory of freedom is not based on freedom to do as we chose, in either of the two senses discussed, what then the freedom is? Sartre discusses in the "BEING AND NOTHINGNESS", He says 'the fundamental act of freedom is .... A choice of myself in the world and by the same token it is a discovery of the world".

Sartre, on the other hand maintains that freedom is a choice of man, he chooses himself in-this very world and thus discovers the world too. Men are free in the sense that they can choose themselves to the extent of choosing the 'self' they would like to be. In other words of saying that man strives for choosing ideal self; and unless he has realized his ideal self; his freedom is not complete. His freedom is complete only on the sense if he is able to realize the ideal self. Though man may not attain success while realizing the ideal self yet he cannot afford, not to try this realization. But true ideal self is indeed unrealizable. Sartre on the other hand maintains that though man is free in making choices yet he is not that much free to choose what he is. That means it is not in man's hand to choose freely, the state of his present circumstances, under which he exists. In other words of saying, man has to accept his present existence simply in the same condition of what he is without any options and without any alterations.

Summarizing, it can be said that freedom still remains the central concern of Sartre's entire philosophy. There could be only two stand points on human freedom which are essential. (I) Human beings are free to choose themselves in the sense of choosing the "self" they want to be. (II) Human beings are not in the least free to choose, what they are.

Thus, it can be said that human beings have freedom and they are responsible for what they are. To conclude it can be said that Sartre has not changed his mind regarding freedom and responsibility.

---

*Refers: (THE LITERATURE OF POSSIBILITY, HAZEL E. BERNES, Tavistock Pub. 1959, P. 284)

** (BEING AND NOTHINGNESS, JP SARTRE, P. 488)

*** (BEING AND NOTHINGNESS, JP SARTRE, P. 489),

**** (BEING AND NOTHINGNESS, JP SARTRE, P. 437),

***** (BEING AND NOTHINGNESS, JP SARTRE,P. 453),

****** (BEING AND NOTHINGNESS, JP SARTRE, P. 436-437)

(BEING AND NOTHINGNESS, JP SARTRE, P. 483)

(BEING AND NOTHINGNESS, JP SARTRE, P. 615)

(BEING AND NOTHINGNESS, JP SARTRE, P. 328)

CHAPTER L

SARTRE'S ATHEISM

Before entering into discussion on Sartre's atheism, it will be better to give Kierkegaard's views on God in order to make a distinction between the first theistic existentialist and the last atheistic existentialist.

Kierkegaard, being the theistic existentialist was fully devoted to God. He very much believed in the existence of God and had full faith in Him. He believed that man has that inherent capacity by which he can enter into bonds of commitment to God. Life lived in devotion to God and in pursuit of moral life is the ethico-religious stage of human existence. Man makes choice. And in choosing he chooses the ethico-religious existence and enters upon an inward commitment to God and thereby realizes that he is an 'existing' individual.

Man faces and accepts despair in his ethico-religious stage of existence. Despair discloses to him his isolation and separation from God. Hence out of despair he takes an existential leap to faith in God, least he should succumb to sickness unto death. Faith in God is thus a "life necessity". In the ethico-religious stage of existence, man commits himself to inward decision and responsible action with earnestness and passion and enters into bonds of commitment to God. But man is not able to sustain himself always in God-relationship, and hence arises his religious suffering which is due to the inevitable moments of separation from God. However, suffering only intensifies his feeling for God and leads him into closer bonds with him.

Sartre's philosophy is atheistic and his views of commitment, is non-religious, social and political. He does not believe in "existence of God". He also regards faith in Good as contradictory to human freedom and responsibility.

Though Sartre's account of his loss of faith sounds light hearted enough, his atheism is something that is very serious and important to him. As he has said, it is extremely important that God does not exists. * And he is contemptuous of those who simply cease believing. The non-existence of God leaves man on his own and he finds this terrifying but it also puts man in full possession of his freedom and forces him to face up to the fact that he is totally responsible for himself.

This is in fact one of the main themes of what is perhaps Sartre's most powerful play, written in 1952 "THE DEVIL AND THE GOOD LORD". Its main character, Goetz realizes that human existence is not a matter of either pure evil or pure good, but an ambiguous mixture of good and evil. It is not a matter of choosing either God or the devil, either Heaven or hell. It is a matter of choosing man as he is, and the earth as it is. Goetz cries, God does not exist; joy, tears of joy; no more heaven, no more hell; nothing but earth".

The following lines will further reveal the death of God as announced by Goetz to the bad priest Heinrich. Goetz tells that "He sent messages to heaven but come no reply. Heaven ignored his very existence. Now that he knows that answer and declared that God does not see, hear, and know him, silence, absence and the loneliness of man is God. Man, alone invents good and decides on evil. Goetz further says that "Man is nothing; if man exists.... God is no more. **

Summarizing, it can be said that what is important for Sartre's position is not the disproof of God's existence but; much more simply, the absence of any belief in his existence. It is one's faith only which matters; since it is almost impossible to prove the existence of God. Kierkegaard along with other theistic existentialists had faith in God, therefore God existed although none of them could prove the existence of God. Yet they continued with their faith in him and lived a life of religious-faith. For Kierkegaard, it was a matter of great faith only which made him such a great theistic philosopher. He propounded a theory of either/or and in choosing he had chosen the ethico-religious life and lived throughout his life in relationship with God.

Granted, on whatever grounds, the logical impossibility of the traditional God; that is, for a Kierkegaard, just the reason to foster our faith in him. Logical impossibility can no more conquer faith than logical possibility can create it. *** What matters, then, is not the inaccessibility of God to logic but the actual fact that I do not believe in him.

---

* Sartre in the 'EXISTENTIALISM IS A HUMANISM", interprets the concept of "abandonment" as the doctrine of atheism. Sartre says by "abandonment", he means to say that God does not exist, and that it is necessary to draw the consequences of his absence right to the end....". (FROM RATIONALISM TO EXISTENTIALISM, SOLOMON ROBERTT C, P. 284-286)

** Refers (THE EXISTENTIALIST AND JP SARTRE, MAX CHARL SWORTH, P 83)

*** Introduction to Existentialism, Grene Marjorie, P. 43)

COMPARATIVE AND EVALUATIVE STUDY ON THOUGHTS OF THEISTIC AND ATHEISTIC EXISTENTIALISTS

CHAPTER LI

COMPARISON

So far, the views of some great theistic and atheistic existentialist philosophers such as Kierkegaard, Jaspers, Nietzsche, Marcel, Sartre etc. have been discussed. We had to discuss them just as they are in their diversity and particularity, and some of us might wonder whether they are not so different as human beings, so particular in their language and thought and sometimes so antagonistic to each other that one is unable to see why they have in common, 'even if we agree to call them existentialists one may object'. We fail to see what that existentialism is on which they agree. There is not one philosophy which can be called existentialism, but several philosophies with wide differences come under this title. It is not even possible to make a clear-cut distinction between German Philosophers of existence and French existentialists. Sartre is nearer to Heidegger than to Marcel, and Heidegger would like to form a class of his own as 'existentialist'. There is no set of principles common to them all, nor do they share well defined methods comparable to the dialect of Hegelians. Nevertheless, they belong together. They are faced with same challenge to which they have to respond, and are involved in the same predicament. Though their answers are not identical, they move in parallel directions and are even if opposed to each other, internally related. In other words, the term "existentialism" points to a certain state of mind, to a specific approach or attitude to a spiritual movement which is of significance in present circumstances and to a specific mode of thought, in any case to something which is alive. The philosophy of existence is philosophy of liberation rather than philosophy of freedom. Existentialists attempt to liberate man from the domination of external forces, of society, of the state, and of the dictatorial power. They want to set free man's authentic self from the shackles of inauthentic self.[1]

The main difference between the philosophy of Kierkegaard and Karl Jaspers lies in this that Kierkegaard makes a choice, chooses to be a Christian, and in order to consummate his choice, comes to recognize another factor- the grace of God. Karl Jaspers, on the other hand, merely puts before us the variable choices, the different viewpoints that different men have had, and defines existence in terms of choice, rather than commit him-self to any particular choice. Thus, where Kierkegaard and Nietzsche have definite viewpoints, Jaspers influenced as he is by them., strives to put before us all the various possible viewpoints, rather than his own particular one.

Gabriel Marcel was not particularly influenced by Kierkegaard, although in certain respects his position has paralleled Kierkegaard. His chief concern is to overcome conceptual oppositions-oppositions of subject and object, thought and being, body and soul, so as to arrive at a domain that he calls the domain of mystery in contradiction to the domain of problems.

Kierkegaard's concept of human freedom is based on his faith in God and his faith in man's inherent capacity to enter into bonds of commitment of God. Life is liked in devotion to God and in pursuit of moral life in the ethico-religious stage of human existence. The choice between these levels of human existence is an existential choice which presents itself to each man as an Either/or. Man's whole being is involved in this choice and the choice he makes decides the level of his existence. The either/or express the existential relation between the ethico-religious and the aesthetic levels of existence, either he chooses the ethico-religious existence, enters upon an inward commitment to God and thereby realizes that he is an inward commitment to God and thereby realizes that he is an 'existing' individual, or he completely loses himself in objective pleasures or theoretical speculation and thereby forgets that he is an 'existing' individual. In this 'existential' choice man does not choose anything outside him-self, but chooses himself either to exist as a unique individual or not exist. So, since man chooses himself in the existential choice either one way or the other, the existential choice essentially connects the reality of the act of choice rather than the object of choice.

Either man is faced with the choice between the two levels of being; either to be present in the world as a 'thing' thrown into it or to exist as a man conscious of his freedom and responsibility. The former level of being is the inauthentic mod of being-there in which man mostly discloses the kind of being he is as a living thing, consciousness and mind. The later level of being is the authentic mode of being-oneself in which man discloses his existence, subjectivity and freedom. It is the authentic personal existence of the one who consciously distinguishes himself from the rest of the world, realizes himself as a 'freedom' capable of choice and activity, and accepts responsibility for all his decisions, actions and convictions.

Kierkegaard's negative attitude to life and his emphasis on man's commitment to God as more essential to authentic existence than man's commitment to his fellow-beings is peculiar to Kierkegaard's philosophy and are not shared by Marcel and Jaspers in spite of their general indebtness to Kierkegaard. They place an equal emphasis on man's commitment to both God and man and maintain that man's moral relations with others in the world constitute the ground of the spiritual efforts towards God realization or transcendence.

In basing the life of freedom on faith in God, Kierkegaard differs from Sartre and Heidegger. For Sartre and Heidegger, freedom of human existence implies the life of man oriented towards the realization of one's own inherent potentiality of-being through personal choices; theirs is an earth-bound concept of freedom and transcendence, it means, man's passing from the present state of his being-in-the-world to its future state by exercising his own personal decision in the process. Both Sartre and Heidegger propound a philosophy of human finiteness and limit the significance of the life of freedom to an existence which is temporal and finite. But Kierkegaard regards the self as a synthesis of the finite and the infinite, the temporal and the eternal, and conceives the life of freedom as an unfolding of its capacity for infinite love and eternal happiness by transcending one's egocentric limitations. The life of freedom is oriented towards an inward personal relationship with God, who is transcendent and eternal and not towards the realization of one's worldly possibilities.

Unlike Sartre and Heidegger, Kierkegaard maintains that the 'despair' which is the outcome of inauthentic existence can be accepted and faced by the individual only by turning towards God and cultivating faith in Him, otherwise he will succumb to sickness unto death. Sartre, an atheistic existentialist regards faith in God as contradictory of human freedom and responsibility. Kierkegaard regards it as the conditions and support of human freedom. In this respect, the view of Kierkegaard resembles the view of Jaspers, another theistic existentialist who also maintains that the life of freedom can be sustained only by one's hope and faith in transcendence.

Like Sartre and Heidegger, Kierkegaard recognizes the close relation of the individual's conception of death to his life of freedom. The anticipation of death makes a difference to all his decisions and transforms his life from inauthentic to authentic existence. But Kierkegaard does not believe, like Heidegger and Sartre, atheistic existentialists, that human existence is reduced to 'nothingness' and becomes worthless in the face of its annihilation in death. He maintains that t acquires an infinite worth in as much as it participates in an inward God-relationship. Authentic life of the individual is ultimately purposeless, as Sartre believes but has the supreme purpose of entering into relationship with God, and this is Kierkegaard's theistic and purposive conception of human freedom.

Gabriel Marcel develops his conception of freedom in close agreement with Kierkegaard's theistic conception of freedom. But he does not share Kierkegaard's negative attitude to life, his emphasis on exclusive 'subjectivity' and man's commitment to God as more essential to his authentic existence tan his commitment to other man. Marcel believes that man's commitment is not only to God but also to other man and that the two commitments are inter-related.

Man's moral relations with others give him a fullness of being which he otherwise lacks and also serves as the medium through which he can enter into relation with God. Man's faith in God, on the other hand, sustains and supports in him the cultivation of the spirit of love, fidelity and service towards his fellowmen and a deviation from this path of commitment would land him in treason. Man's commitment with God is a matter of trust of belief in Him, is an expression of man's faith in him.

Corresponding to the distinction between inauthentic and authentic existence drawn by the other existentialists, Marcel draws a distinction between two kinds of persons.

1. Handy and available
2. Unhandy and unavailable.

The unhandy and unavailable are those who are self-centered and whose existence is 'lost' in the pursuit of their personal desires and pleasures. Because of their selfishness, they are incapable of love, compassion and sacrifice for others.

Distinguished from these are the 'handy' and 'available' who transcend the limitations of their petty ego and activity enter into relations of love, sympathy, and service with others, thereby making themselves 'handy' and 'available' for others.

Man has his structure constituted as being-with-others and he discovers his freedom only as part of this structure. In his conception of man as always involved in the 'world' and not 'abstracted' from it. Marcel agrees with Sartre, Jaspers and Martin Heidegger.

But Marcel distinguishes himself from the other existentialists by his special emphasis on man's being-with-others as expressing the whole truth of human existence. Sartre's view of human existence as basically 'nothingness' and separation; underlies his philosophy of human involvement and activism and invests it with ultimate purposelessness. But Marcel regards the 'separative' view of consciousness as arising out of an abstraction and therefore erroneous, the only basic truth of human existence being its participation.

Unlike Sartre and Heidegger, Marcel believes that human transcendence is not merely 'horizontal' as passing from the present to the future in order of time but is 'vertical' and passing beyond the finite and the temporal to the transcendent and the eternal. The self-transcendence of the finite and temporal human existence takes place only when it enters into bonds of commitment with God, who is transcendent and eternal, and establishes its 'being' in relation to him. Marcel agrees with Kierkegaard in thus emphasizing that man has to enter into a personal relationship of commitment to God, if he is to live an authentic human existence but man cannot commit himself to God without committing himself to his fellow-beings in the same act. The need for man's commitment of his fellow-beings by entering into relations of trust, love and sympathy with them as part of his commitment to God finds special emphasis in the philosophy of Marcel.

As mentioned earlier, freedom and responsibility form the core of existentialism. Kierkegaard, the father of existentialism, says that it is the question of freedom that brings me into conflict with Hegel. Freedom, says Kierkegaard, is man's greatness and grandeur. His charge against Hegel is that he has left no room in his system for our feeling of freedom.

This idea of freedom is also to be found at the center of Jaspers thought. How is it? He asks that we are free, how it is that existence is essentially freedom? It is because transcendence is concealed from us. If transcendence were revealed to us directly, we should not say Jaspers be able to be free. Transcendence would dominate us. Transcendence conceals or veils itself. Transcendence, to use a Kierkegaardian expression taken over by Jaspers, refrains from revealing itself save indirectly so as to put our freedom to the test. Accordingly, the domain of existence is the domain of freedom, and hence that of possibility project and choice. Karl Jaspers wrote in the "REASON AND EXISTENCE" that 'both leaped toward transcendence, but to a form of transcendence where practically no one could follow. Kierkegaard leaped to Christianity which was conceived as an absurd paradox, as decision for utter world negation and martyrdom. Nietzsche leaped to the eternal return and superman.

The similarity of their thoughts is even much more striking precisely than their apparent differences, the Christian belief on the one, and the atheism emphasized by the other. In an epoch of reflection, where what had recently passed away seemed still to endure, but which actually lives in an absence of faith-rejecting faith and forcing oneself to believe belong together. The godless can appear to be a believer, the believer can appear as godless both stand in the same dialectic.

The philosophy of Jean Paul Sartre has many points in common with that of martin Heidegger despite the fact that Sartre has criticized Heidegger in the "BEING AND NOTHINGNESS" and Heidegger has, in his "LETTER OF HUMANISM" elaborated some basic differences which he believes, separate him from Sartre.

The idea of choice, as in Jaspers and Kierkegaard's philosophy, can also be found in the philosophy of Sartre. Sartre insists above all on the fact that it is by my own choice that I create values; I am the unfounded foundation of all values; since I am the one who finds everything. I myself am without foundation; I am the being that brings values into the world and for that very reason I myself am unjustifiable. Sartre, like Kierkegaard, insists that there are no external signs to guide me; I must make my own rules and make them alone.[2]

Sartre's whole thought revolves round the idea of freedom. Freedom, says Sartre, is the main foundation of values; it is true that he lays down a sort of universalization of values. My freedom is inter-dependent with that of all others; nevertheless, my freedom is basically my freedom. No other has to follow the path I follow.

Sartre's doctrine of freedom has a number of peculiar features. To begin with, Sartre maintains that if a being is free, he is always free, in all situations, under all circumstances. In most classical theories of freedom, we are said to be free to certain moments and not free at certain others. But Sartre tells us that if man is free, he is always free. It would be incomprehensible, he argues, that freedom should disappear and reappear at some later moment. Consequently, we are equally free whether we decide to be cowardly or courageous; whichever way act, our responsibility is in no way cut down, on the contrary since in either case there is a choice, in both cases there is decision and freedom and consequent responsibility.

The view that man is equally free at all times is one which had not been previously maintained. It is to Sartre credit to have put forwarded this view which, though tending to destroy the very feeling of freedom that Sartre means to safe guard, offers a new subject for reflection. What is more, freedom always appears in Sartre and in jaspers and Heidegger too, as limitation and finitude. An act of freedom is always an act by which we choose some specific thing. Sartre goes even further; freedom is in a sense a lesser kind of being; it is a deficiency, a lack, a sort of gap, a sort of nothingness within being. What is here involved is Sartre's whole doctrine of the for-it-self, his whole doctrine of nothingness. I am the being that I am not and I am not the being that I am. Freedom is tied up with my essential negativity (in the Hegelian and dialectical sense of the word as well as in the Sartrian sense).

Our freedom is a fact; it is part of our facticity, to use the word used by Heidegger and after him by Sartre. Freedom is not self-determined initially; and as it is part of our facticity, we are not free not to choose, we are free not to choose, we are not free not to be free. This is the import of Sartre's statement that we are condemned to be free. Thus, there is not only a facticity, but also a necessity to our contingency. We might say and this would indicate an internal difficulty in Sartre's thought that it is man's nature to be free but Sartre rejects the idea of nature properly speaking and freedom in fact is not a nature, since it always affords us the possibility of being something other than what we are.

All existentialists start from one point and return to the same. Because the very existence of man on this earth is menaced, because the annihilation of man, his dehumanization and the destruction of his humanity and of all moral values is a real danger, therefore the meaning of human existence becomes our problem. We have to reinterpret man, his position in the universe, his relation to his fellowmen and to God.

Man's position in the universe is unique in that he; as a responding being, becomes answerable for his action. This is the moral aspect of his freedom. Respondeo, ergo sum now means that I am in so far as I accept responsibility for my action. It is quite impossible to discuss here the complex problem of responsibility in its legal, moral and religious aspect. I can only stress that without responsiveness there would be no responsibility. The later may be defined, for brevity's sake, as the conditions of a free agent who is conscious of having acted in a certain way and has the ability to account for his motives. Responsibility implies the feeling of being answerable to somebody for something, i.e., for a course of action which either does or does not conform to a specific rule. It arises, not as total responsibility in total solitude, but as limited-responsibility in specific circumstances or as an absolute responsibility before God.

Sartre is right in stressing the responsibility for others even in solitary decision, but he is wrong in making men responsible for actions they did not do and for situations they did not bring about, and for overloading them with total responsibility. He condemns them to infinite liberty which they are unable to bear.

He claims total and infinite liberty. Where as in fact people are dominated by their emotions and passions, he tries to persuade us that we ourselves have chosen to be jealous or sad; that we have chosen our own being and, in a certain sense, even our coming into this world. De facto, he has mistaken natural spontaneity for moral liberty and understands this spontaneity a nothingness. If we object that he himself took initiative in defining the man as 'liberate, en situation' and this situation implies freedom and sometimes necessity. He replies with utmost confidence that even in prison, in war, or in the hand of a torturer one remains free, because one has chosen to be in that situation. This so-called freedom, which is reality is not freedom at all it is absurd and seems ridiculous.

Kierkegaard and Jaspers too have heavily accented the theme of responsibility for himself and for others. Kierkegaard says that "the self exists authentically when it becomes free to shoulder its responsibility and open itself for a commitment, religiously defined as a commitment to God who commands a resolute love of one's neighbor.[3]

Karl Jaspers writes that in communication "I sense a responsibility not only for myself but also for the other self. **

Heidegger to, makes his DASEIN (Being) responsible for his acts in that particular situation. He says that "Dasein (being) is confronted with the responsibility of determining what significance this situation will have in his future decisions; what role it will play in his project of becoming that being which he is not yet. But this implies that being is in a real sense beyond this situation. He can transcend it in freedom. Being is his own freedom thus becomes responsible for his situation, but at the same time his freedom remains forever a freedom-in-a-situation. The freedom of being is limited and finite.[4]

Nietzsche explicitly denies "human freedom and exhibits a genuine-if philosophical distaste for the "concrete worldly existence" of man. #

Here Nietzsche could be related to Kierkegaard in a sense that "if Kierkegaard is the father of contemporary existentialism, Nietzsche is its tutor, where Kierkegaard is a philosopher of existence, Nietzsche is a philosopher of life and the world".

Regarding the existence of God and responsibility towards him, Nietzsche writes "we deny God, we deny the responsibility in god". ##

Nietzsche finds God an obstacle in the process of realization of human freedom. He writes "Unless God is dead, human freedom is not complete". He further says that "the death of God makes man alone responsible for the values with which he endows the earth.[5]

JP Sartre is right in connecting liberty with responsibility and also in making us responsible for our being, our action and for the universe. He discusses the subject of responsibility in the "BEING AND NOTHINGNESS" and states that ".... The responsibility of the for-itself extends to the entire world as a people-world". ### He even holds man responsible for the world war and reaches the startling conclusion that "man being condemned to be free carried the load of the whole world on his shoulders and is responsible for the world and for himself in his specific being. This sounds wonderful, but what does it amount to?

"Responsibility" here has a merely naturalistic concept namely "consciousness of being the incontestable author of an event or of an object". It simply means that homo-creator or rather man the would-be—creator, regards himself as the author of things. In this sense he is naturally responsible but he is not "morally responsible"; he is not answerable either to God who does not exists, nor to a moral law or to values which are denied objective validity and depend on the individual as their creator. Sartre maintains that whatever happens is "mine" and that no happening is "inhuman".

---

*Refers (BEING AND NOTHINGNESS, JP SARTRE, P. 558, 59)

**Refers (PHILOSOPHIE, KARL JASPERS, VOL II P. 334)

Refers (EXISTENTIALISM AS PHILOSOPHY, FERNADO MOLINA, PRENTICE HALL, IN, 1962, P.2)

##Refers (A TROCHHI's "THE OUTSIDERS", P. 501, Italics Mine)

###Refers (BEING AND NOTHINGNESS, JP SARTRE, TR BY HAZEL BARNES, NEW YORK 1956, P. 556)

CHAPTER LII

REVIEW

The philosophy that is at present known as existentialism is identified mainly with the names of Kierkegaard, Karl Jaspers, M. Gabriel, Heidegger and Sartre etc. It is fundamentally pessimistic-even nihilistic and a limit seems to have been reached in its development. For a quite few years, there has been no new contribution. Kierkegaard's "UNSCIENTIFIC POSTSCRIPT", Heidegger's "BEING AND TIME" and Sartre's "BEING AND NOTHINGNESS" remains standard works that have not been superseded. Existentialism seems to have come to a grinding halt.

It seems to be generally accepted that Existentialism is necessary a philosophy of pessimism-or at least, of a very limited, stoical kind of optimism.

What is usually meant by existentialism- the philosophy that began with Kierkegaard and later represented by Karl Jaspers, Martin Heidegger, Marcel, Nietzsche, and JP Sartre – is no longer a living philosophy. It has run itself into a "cul de sac" (Saturation), and there is no chance of further development. But this is not to say that existentialism is dead; only that in its Kierkegaard-Sartre form it has reached a point from which it can neither advance nor retreat. But a new more interesting form of existentialism can be developed that avoids this cul de sec, and that can continue to develop.

Now going one by one from Kierkegaard to Sartre, we will critically examine and see how far they contributed towards the development of existentialism.

Kierkegaard must be understood largely as a philosopher in revolt. Most of what Kierkegaard had to say is irrelevant to the twentieth century. He was too religious, but the absurdities and excess of Kierkegaard's philosophy are less important than the urge behind them, the agonized thirst for meaning that was only partly the result of neurotic mala-adjustment and sexual frustration, it is this thirst for meaning and makes Kierkegaard relevant to our own time.

Karl Jaspers too cannot be easily summarized, his thoughts move in great sweeps, and his meanings only begin to emerge after one has read a hundred pages or so. But what is clear is the pessimistic tone of his thought. Man encountering his true self only in the boundary situations of existence, death, suffering, guilt, and the sudden violent accidents.

One feels finally of Jaspers that he has clearly grasped the need for a new kind of philosophy, a new way for man to grasp his knowledge, but he has spent most of his time and strength in trying to explain how the situation has come about. His thoughts seem to move on the slippery ground of the existential paradox; that to live is the opposite of to know; so human knowledge can never grasp human existence. It must always falsify it. This is the paradox that defeated Kierkegaard, Jaspers difficult terminology is inadequate for conveying the living, complicated stuff of human existence, Karl Jaspers must be judged a failure.

By this criterion, the same must be said of Martin Heidegger. His temperament is close to that of Kierkegaard in reading Heidegger, one is constantly aware of his rejection of the 'hard'. Jaspers basic obsession is the great sweep of all human thought. Heidegger is the poet, standing apart from society, and receiving sudden flashes of insight into the true nature of human existence. He can never communicate these insights to the herd because of this very nature of the herd. It's tendency to look around continually at the rest of the herd and to live in other people's eyes. The driving force behind civilization is the vital impulses or the men who stand alone.

Because of this feeling of the immense difficulty of saying anything important, Heidegger, like, Jaspers, makes very heavy weather of the business of communication; in fact, he is the most obscure of modern philosophers.

Nevertheless, his central insight is easy to express. Man is a strange, inauthentic creature who has very little contact with real existence. Intellectuals cut themselves off from reality by trapping themselves off from the reality by trapping themselves in a world of concepts ordinary men are cut from reality because they are so self-absorbed, so involved in the pettiness of everyday existence. They live in a meaningless world because they find it so difficult to mean anything. This is the trouble "forgetfulness of existence". The problem is somehow to get back to existence. Like Jaspers, Heidegger does not seem too very sure. He devotes a great deal of analysis to the in-authenticity of the herd and his every day existence. He recognizes that man often springs into 'authentic existence' when confronted with death, and that poets often become aware of it without this stimulus.

But as with Kierkegaard, we feel that Heidegger is important because of something he felt rather than anything he thought. The drive behind the work is the same hunger for meaning, which he identifies with existence. He tries to use language in an oddly stilted, clumsy way. Thus, he also falls into Jasper's category.

Gabriel Marcel called a theistic existentialist stressed the concrete over the abstract and the mystery of being. His philosophy is a departure from the general trend of continental existentialism as represented especially by the works of Martin Heidegger, JP Sartre, portrays human existence as a futile mode of being characterized by finitude and burdened with care and the enmity of others. Marcel's existentialism is an experiential philosophy in which the exigencies of being human are mitigated by the individual's invocation of God. The pivotal thesis of Marcel's philosophy is 'easest coesse" to be is to be others. The concrete manifestation of this thesis is the inter-subjective nexus, human and divine.

Along with other forms of existentialism Marcel's philosophy is intrinsically limited by its reliance on the phenomenological method. This is simply the description of phenomena-objects and stated of consciousness as they appear to the apprehending subject. Such a method excludes deduction and a priori reasoning, the better to guarantee the close alliance of being and knowing.

This necessarily limits the observer to his own personal experiences into the universal experiences of all mankind.

Nietzsche's views on the will to power and his concepts of superman have attracted criticism from different quarters. Nietzsche's entire moral philosophy rests on the psychological principle referred as the will to power. What Nietzsche means by "der willezumacht" (will to power) is not easily understood, first because the notion of 'power' is so often taken in the sense of physical or military power, is so often taken and encouraged by Nietzsche's frequent appeal to military allegories in his writings, secondly, because the role and the meaning of the will to power changed significantly in the course of Nietzsche's career. The confusion resulting from Nietzsche's several changes in his concept of the will to power has led several commentators to dismiss the notion from Nietzsche's thought.

The interpretation of will to power as a purely political notion is simply inconsistent with demands made by Nietzsche throughout his works. The phrase "will to power" appears late in Nietzsche's writings, and then not at first as the most celebrated principle of his philosophy.

Lastly, we can say the excitement of Nietzsche's philosophy is ultimately, essentially negative; the will to power does not so much give us a new standard, but makes explicit the standard; we have always used. The radical conclusions of Nietzsche's philosophy are not so much the result of his offering us a replacement for traditional values, rather he tries to show us that these traditional values are inconsistent.

Nietzsche's will to power is far removed from the common imaginary of military strength the most powerful are not the politicians and soldiers, but the artists, the philosophers and the aesthetics. Will to power is control over one's self; it is not license but restrain it; not power to hurt or destroy but power to create.

Now assessing his views on superman, we can emphatically say that Nietzsche's vision of the superman is one of the most fascinating aspects of his philosophy, as well as the most misinterpreted. With the doctrine of superman, we get the other half of Nietzsche's theory of man-man understood as possibility.

Initially, Nietzsche certainly believed that his new teaching of the superman could fill the void, that he was providing man with a creed which could replace the old religion. Gradually, however he realized that his teachings are not a remedy, but a further contributory force to decadence and destruction.

Commenting on Nietzsche's superman, Karl Jaspers emphasizes the distinction between the superior men have already appeared in history, but the superman has not yet arrived.

Nietzsche's concept of the superman may be contrasted with Aurobindo concept of, the superman. Aurobindo believes that a new human society will be evolved by spiritually transformed men or supermen, who will completely surrender their will to the divine will, eschew love and hatred transcend egoism, rise above intellect and intellectual morality, identify themselves with mankind, and become conscious instruments of the will and energy of God. They will work with the super-mind, and bring down the kingdom of God on earth. This concept may seem to be utopian and unrealizable, but Aurobindo believes that it is inescapable and irresistible.

Nietzsche credited himself of being the first atheistic existentialist and completely denied the role of God in human life. He postulated "we deny god, we deny the responsibility in God" and at other places he says "unless God is dead, human freedom is not complete". Thus, we see that for Nietzsche the death of God makes man alone responsible for the values with which he endows the earth. Of course, "God is dead, God has died" are obviously not the statement of a straightforward atheist. The atheist would simply say that there is no God, that believe in him is a nonsensical superstition and has no foundation whatever; but the phrase "God id dead" refers to the loss of faith.

Sartre, for purpose of expositions, remains the best representative of the modern existentialist tradition. All its problems and its faults can be seen most clearly in his work. His work also makes it plain why existentialism has advanced so little after Kierkegaard.

The first thing to note about Sartre is that his temperament is naturally gloomy and pessimistic. Like Heidegger, he is preoccupied with the fact that the world "exists" quite apart from our minds, but he seems to find this separate existence disquieting or even nauseating.

Sartre is as much pre-occupied as Heidegger with man's in-authenticity as a social being, with mediocrity of life in the eyes of other people, is the obverse side of Heidegger's observations about the poet and solitude. He agrees heartily with Dostoevsky that it is impossible to love you fellow men if you have much contact with him; but solitude is no answer; it is likely to lead to nauseas.

In Heidegger's form, existentialism can still be optimistic, man deliberately detaches himself to overcome reality turning it into an abstraction, a mere instrument of his will; then through poetry or meditation on death, he again returns to existence, and is revitalized. He gets the best of both worlds. For Sartre, there could be no escape; the choice was between the in-authenticity of people and the nausea of things.

We may decipher well from the following paragraphs that why existentialism is a failure?

Existentialism was a philosophy of man without an organized religion. This is not to say a philosophy of man without God. Many existentialists have believed in God. But there could be no confronting intermediary or savior. Man stood alone if God existed, then the lonely individual head to find him without help. It started with romanticism; Kierkegaard and Nietzsche were as much romantics as existentialist, but Jaspers, Heidegger, and Sartre and the rest wrote as thinkers rather than as poets. With them, existentialism became an intellectualized romanticism. It had a tougher quality than its nineteenth century predecessor and instead of ending in nostalgia and defeat, it has ended in stoicism and defeat.

Existentialism, like romanticism, is a philosophy of freedom and responsibility. It has reached a stand still because no existential thinker can agree that there are any values outside man- that is outside man's ordinary, everyday consciousness. Man is free, says Sartre. But what he is to do with his freedom? He can do anything he likes, Sartre replies, but then, just as every body's business is no body's business, so freedom for anything is freedom for nothing. Man is free, but the world is empty and meaningless. This is the problem, while this sentence remains a summary of existentialism, there is nothing further to be done.

To summarize, it can be said that Existentialism has pointed out a series of problems but has offered no solution, partly because the problems are do complex and many-sided that no simple solution is possible and partly because they are to a certain extent, in principle insoluble. Now we see clearly that "Existentialist system", Existentialist logic" and "Existentialist ontology" have no meaning in the present perspective. In other words, we can say that they are dead. Apart from this, even, existentialists have failed in providing a new basis to ethics and for a theory of value. And it will not be out of place to mention here that existentialism has not even provided a basis for a new humanism (though, Sartre might claim sometimes that existentialism does provide a basis). But apart from everything else, the existentialism yet forms the core of human liberty and responsibility and it provokes one to think of it.

CHAPTER LIII

CONCLUSION

I have tried to present the core of existentialism, by discussing the freedom and responsibility constituted by the actual descriptions made by existentialists of the essential structures of human existence. It had focused our attention on human nature and existence.

To conclude, existentialists center of thinking remains man and they continue to consider human existence, as their subject of thinking in this world.

Most of the existentialists have maintained in their discussions that philosophers of the past overlooked the most passing problems of man and of human existence.

Existentialism started as a movement and it seems as if after the death of last existentialist, JP Sartre, in 1980; this movement seems to have lost the enthusiasm and the vigor with which it was started in forties. Now, there is a need, again to restart with full zeal in order to keep it alive as this movement concerns with the very ingredients of human life, that is, the freedom and responsibility. My efforts have been to re-evaluate the whole thing and present the human liberty and responsibility without any bias.

In the present circumstances, the function of existentialism should be to bring about a revaluation of problems and to liberate us from certain traditional problems; whether they are material or purely formal and technical.

Human figure presented by these philosophers (from Kierkegaard to JP Sartre) to a larger extent, though with certain basic differences, revolves round the authentic and inauthentic existence. To a greater extent it does not seem logical to see that total human existence or humanity is just being divided in the two categories of beings, i.e., "Authentic and the inauthentic". Thus, depriving the inauthentic persons of authenticity in span of their life. Even authentic men may turn inauthentic in due course of time and vice-versa. Here, distinguishing the authentic from inauthentic and bringing out a third category of being i.e., "semi-authentic existence" where man has a certain percentage of logical possibility of being drifting either side. It seems irrational to place a new born child (at the moment who is not concerned at all with freedom and responsibility) straight into authentic category of existence. If he starts from authentic mode of human existence, i.e., thrown into the world (as Kierkegaard maintains it) and exists as a human being throughout his life as inauthentic person, or the second possibility of choosing or entering into "semi-authentic existence" category of human existence and staying throughout or becoming rather turning authentic human being realizing the freedom and responsibility. The reason for stressing this third category of human existence is that for an inauthentic human being it is very difficult to enter straight into authentic category of human existence. It has to follow a channel i.e., "inauthentic-semi-authentic- authentic mode of human existence.

Each man is thus faced with the choice among the three levels of being; either to be present in the world as a thing thrown into it or to be progressing rather on its way in becoming authentic or to exist as a being conscious of his freedom and responsibility.

The first level of being is the inauthentic mode of being there in which man mostly discloses the kind of being he is as a living thing and in the second level i.e., semi-authentic level of existence; he is conscious of becoming authentic and having mind that means he is a man who can disclose himself with consciousness and mind; and the third level of being is the authentic mode of being-one-self in which man discloses his existence, subjectivity and freedom. It is the authentic personal existence of the man who consciously distinguishes himself from the rest of the world, realizes his "freedom". Man becomes capable of choice and activity, and accepts responsibility for all his decisions, actions and convictions.

Generally, it is believed that existentialism is pessimistic in its outlook; but what is the source of this pessimism? I think the limitation of human consciousness is the source of all pessimism. Consciousness is the freedom which is intentional in its nature. Freedom in itself as no import only the feeling of freedom or consciousness of freedom has a great import in human life. Our life is a continual act of choice. Choice is nothing but an act of selected certain sets of facts in accordance with one's mood, values and ideals. In our day-to-day life we make choices. Existentialism helps us in making right choices. Today we need existentialism to develop as a strong philosophy which is more immediate and personal. Existentialism should, thus, be primarily concerned not with "all men" collectively but with "each man" distributely. Existentialism should continue to emphasize individual freedom and responsibility.

In the modern context, the human freedom presented by existentialist thinkers is logical only to the extent, as long as they hold man to be a responsive animal.

Man could be defined as the responsive animal i.e., as that being in which the responsiveness of organic beings reaches its highest peak and its widest applications. He possesses the whole range of responses from automatic, instinctive, unconscious, involuntary, to conditioned, ideomotor, and voluntary unit responses. He beats the animal by being able to alter the modes of his response i.e., by learning, by responding to sign, and with their help to imaginary or non-existent objects, and by formulating his conscious responses in answers, i.e., by speech.

Man's position in the universe is unique in that he; as a responding being, becomes answerable for his actions. This is the moral aspect of his freedom, and freedom implies responsibility. Man, alone could be held responsible for his acts. Under no circumstances he can be held responsible for he acts he did not do. A man is responsible for his actions because in acting he acts in his own, unique situation, into which he may bring his fellows interests or he may not. He may withdraw from his place in society if he so desires, and thus his responsibility for what he does in society is a relation between his own situation and those of others who are affected by his actions.

If a man recognizes that he is responsible for what he does, that he is in relation with others, and that he can construct his situation in his own way, and if his responsibility for what he does is recognized and allowed for by others, then he is free to choose whatever actions are feasible in the circumstances.

A man is responsible for his actions because it is he and no others who constructs the situation in which action takes place, and in terms of which it carries significance.

Almost all the existentialists are unanimous in holding man responsible for his acts. They are right, including Sartre, in stressing the responsibility for others even in solitary decision, but Sartre is wrong in making men responsible for the actions they did not do and for situations they did not create or bring about, and for overloading them with total responsibility. It is extreme, illogical and un-psychological.

In my opinion, the individual must assume responsibility for his society and has a duty to work for its improvement. No social state is a priori worthy; all societies are in need of improvement and I feel always that there is a room for improvement; the social state of static perfection is illusory.

The pragmatic conception of responsibility is awareness of the consequences of one's actions and the choice of alternatives that promise problem solving consequences.

In my opinion, there is little need to expatiate on the fact that the question of human responsibility i.e., the question whether human beings are the true authors of their doings and may be held morally accountable for them, is one which involves the whole structure of the human personality and its relation to the outside world.

The word personality describes that which is personal; that which belongs to one human being. Personality entirely depends upon one's attitude towards life, called one's "Life style". It is by using the abilities derived through heredity and the impressions acquired from one's environment that one builds up one's life style.

A man cannot become the person he wants to be merely by thinking about himself, but only by doing something with himself. This requires involving himself in the affairs of others, in adapting himself to social pressures, in transforming his environment.

Thus, a good personality is one in which all the potentialities of the individual are fully realized. To achieve this one should freely associate with one's fellow men and co-operate whole-heartedly with them.

A person who lives a life apart from his fellow cannot be imbued with the warming and creative influence of love, an essential of any kind of good personality, cannot be sympathetic, cannot be interested in nor interesting to anyone but himself.

The person who is personally responsible for his actions, grows into his personality, in the social life of the family and becomes free to act only as becoming simultaneously the subject of the obligation of duty.

Personality, is the form in which it is supposed to be most intensely, a communion of will and character, a communion of intelligence and mind, a communion of love, implying that each person is, in these various phases or aspects of personal life, capable of complete communion with others.

Personality in the individual is the capacity for society, fellowship and communion; but personality is not a part of society, as it is not part of race. The problem of man, that is to say, the problem of personality, is more primary than the problem of society. All the sociological doctrines about man are erroneous, they know only the superficial, objectified stratum in man, but only an existential philosophy, and not a sociological philosophy, any more than a biological philosophy can construct the true doctrine of man as personality.

Thus, it can be said that existentialism helps man to form his true personality. This is possible only for those human beings who are authentic and at the same time, conscious of their freedom and responsibility.

Existentialist's philosophy thus, very vigorously inspires to do something and be something.

Bibliography

CHAPTER ONE

1. Existentialism and humanism, Karl Jaspers, P.7
2. The Existentialist and JP Sartre, Max Charls Worth, P.P. 8, 71
3. From Hegel to Existentialism, Solomon Robert C, P.P. 243-244
4. Existentialism, JP Sartre, P. 15
5. Existentialism, Paul Foulquie, P.P. 62-65
6. A dictionary of philosophy, A.R. Lacey, P. 79
7. A dictionary of philosophy, Antony Flew, P.125
8. Dialectical materialism, Alexander Spirkin, Progress Publishers, Moscow, P.P. 306-313
9. Dialectical materialism, Alexander Spirkin, Progress Publishers, Moscow, P.P. 314-318

CHAPTER TWO

1. Existentialism, Mary Warnock, Oxford University press, P.P. 6-8
2. Existentialism- for and against, Paul Roubiczek, BKS Demand UMI, P.P. 99-100
3. Existentialism, Mary Warnock, Oxford University Press, P. 11
4. Existentialism- for and against, Paul Roubiczek, BKS Demand UMI, P.P. 100-106
5. Kierkegaard, Hannay Alastair, P.P. 99-100
6. Six Existentialist thinkers, HJ Blackham, London, Routledge & Kegan Paul, P. P. 4-5
7. Existentialism- for and against, Paul Roubiczek, BKS Demand UMI, P.P. 106
8. Kierkegaard's Journals and Papers, Howard V. Hong & Edna, H. Hong, P. 463
9. Existentialism- A theory of man, Cambridge, Mass Harvard University, 1949, Ralph Harper, P.P. 53-54
10. Existentialism, Mary Warnock, Oxford University press, P.P. 12-13
11. From Rationalism to Existentialism, the existentialist and their 19th century background, Solomon Robert C. P. 102
12. From Rationalism to Existentialism, the existentialist and their 19th

century background, Solomon Robert C. P. 89-92
13. From Rationalism to Existentialism, the existentialist and their 19th century background, Solomon Robert C. P. 98-99
14. Kierkegaard thoughts, Gregor Malantschuk, P. 269
15. Existentialism -for and against, Paul Roubiczek, BKS Demand UMI, P. 105
16. Reason and Existenz Tr. by Whilliam Earle, Karl Jasper, P. 35
17. Existentialism, Paul Foulquie, P.P. 104-105

CHAPTER THREE

1. Six Existentialist thinkers, HJ Blackham, London, Routledge and Kegan Paul, Ltd. 1951, P.P. 43-44
2. A short history of Existentialism, Jean Wahl, New York philosophical Library, P.P. 09-10
3. Karl Jaspers- An introduction to his philosophy, Wallraft Charles, F.P. 93
4. Six Existentialist thinkers, HJ Blackham, London, Routledge and Kegan Paul, Ltd. 1951, P.P. 45-48
5. Reason and Existenz Tr. by Whilliam Earle, Karl Jasper, P. 10
6. The perennial scope of philosophy, Ralph Manheim, P. 62
7. Philosophical faith and Revelation, Karl Jaspers, Tr. By E. B. Ashton, P.95
8. Karl Jaspers- An introduction to his philosophy, Wallraft Charles, F.P. 113
9. Philosophie, Vol II, Karl Jaspers, P. 334
10. Man in the modern age, Karl Jaspers, by Eden & Ceder Paul, P. 307
11. Man in the modern age, Karl Jaspers, by Eden & Ceder Paul, P. 188-190
12. Six Existentialist thinkers, HJ Blackham, London, Routledge and Kegan Paul, Ltd. 1951, P.P. 56-58

CHAPTER FOUR

1. Six Existentialist thinkers, HJ Blackham, London, Routledge and Kegan Paul, Ltd. 1951, P.P. 66-67
2. Being and Having- An Existentialist diary, Tr. By Peter Smith, P.P. vi-x
3. Being and Having- An Existentialist diary, Tr. By Peter Smith, P.P. ix
4. The Existentialist background of Human dignity, Gabriel Marcel, BKS

Demand UMI, P.P. 150-152

5. Being and Having- An Existentialist diary, Tr. By Peter Smith, P.P. 172
6. Six Existentialist thinkers, HJ Blackham, London, Routledge and Kegan Paul, Ltd. 1951, P.P. 78
7. The Existentialist concepts and the Hindu philosophical system, G. Srinivasan, P. 185

CHAPTER FIVE

1. Existentialism -for and against, Paul Roubiczek, BKS Demand UMI, P. 29
2. Nietzsche and Christianity, Karl Jaspers P. 47
3. Beyond Good and Evil, Nietzsche Friederich Wilhelm, P. 55
4. Existentialism, A survey and ancient Indian thought, K. Guru Dutt P. 21
5. Nietzsche, Richard Schact, P.P. 304-305
6. Freedom and Karl Jaspers Philosophy, Young Bruehl Elisabeth, P. 72
7. A manual of ethics, Jadunath Sinha, The central book agency, Calcutta, 1960 P. 249
8. The Existentialist concept and the Hindu philosophical system, G. Srinivasan P. 203
9. Nietzsche- Richard Schacht, P.P. 306-309
10. A manual of ethics, Jadunath Sinha, The central book agency, Calcutta, 1960 P. 256-258
11. From Rationalism to Existentialism, the existentialist and their 19th century background, Solomon Robert C. P.P. 127-130
12. The study of philosophy, Will Durant, P. 461

CHAPTER SIX

1. Martin Heidegger on being Human, Richard Schmitt, P.P. 190-192
2. From Rationalism to Existentialism, the existentialist and their 19th century background, Solomon Robert C. P. 219-223
3. Existential Ethics, Warnock Mary, P.P. 13-14
4. Studies in Christian existentialism, John Macquarrie, P.P. 51-52
5. Six Existentialist thinkers, HJ Blackham, London, Routledge and Kegan Paul, Ltd. 1951, P.P. 52-53

CHAPTER SEVEN

1. To freedom condemned, Justus Streller, P.P. 10-12
2. To freedom condemned, Justus Streller, P. 123
3. Existentialism (French) Tr. By Kathleen Raine, Foulquie Paul P. 69
4. Six Existentialist thinkers, HJ Blackham, London, Routledge and Kegan Paul, Ltd. 1951, P.123
5. To freedom condemned, Justus Streller, P.41
6. Six Existentialist thinkers, HJ Blackham, London, Routledge and Kegan Paul, Ltd. 1951, P.136
7. The philosophy of Sartre, Warneck Mary, P.P. 43-45
8. From Rationalism to Existentialism, the existentialist and their 19th century background, Solomon Robert C. P. 278
9. Existentialism -for and against, Paul Roubiczek, BKS Demand UMI, P.P. 126-128
10. Existentialism and human emotions, Jean Paul Sartre, Carol Pub Group, P. 59

CHAPTER EIGHT

1. Existentialism and the modern predicament by F.H. Heinemann, London Adam & Charles Black, 1953, P. 167
2. Philosophy of existence, Jean Wahl, Routledge & Kegan Paul, 1969, P. 59
3. Existence and freedom towards and ontology of human finitude, Calvin O Schrag, North western U. Pr. P. 49
4. Existence and freedom towards and ontology of human finitude, Calvin O Schrag, North Western U. Pr. P. 63
5. Existentialism as philosophy, Fernado Molina, Prentice Hall, 1962 P.P. 28, 97

Printed by Libri Plureos GmbH in Hamburg,
Germany